Present Day Truths

Present Day Truths

by Dick Iverson
with Bill Scheidler

Published by City Christian Publishing
9200 NE Fremont • Portland, Oregon 97220

Printed in the United States of America

City Christian Publishing is a ministry of City Bible Church and is dedicated to serving the local church and its leaders through the production and distribution of quality equipping resources. It is our prayer that these materials, proven in the context of the local church, will equip leaders in exalting the Lord and extending His kingdom.

For a free catalog of additional resources from City Christian Publishing, please call 1-800-777-6057 or visit our web site at *www.CityChristianPublishing.com*.

Present Day Truths
© Copyright 1976 by Dick Iverson
ISBN 0-914936-88-3

DEDICATION

*I wish to acknowledge my deepest thanks
and appreciation to Bill Scheidler, an instructor
on the staff of Portland Bible College, for the countless
hours he spent rewriting this present text from the original.*

CONTENTS

INTRODUCTION

In every generation, God specifically moves with a fresh "rhema" from Heaven. The emphasis of the Spirit is very important to the Church in each generation. What is God saying today? The title of this text is "PRESENT DAY TRUTHS". It is taken from *II Peter 1:12* - *"that ye may be established in present truth"*. It is not enough alone to hear what God has said in past generation, though one builds upon that foundation, but it is essential for the Christian to be current with the fresh move of the Spirit as He is speaking today. God wants us to be established in "present truth". The word "establish" means to set fast, to turn resolutely in a certain direction, to be solid, stable. This word is used in a number of places in Scripture, each declaring what God wants to do at that point in the believer's life. It is also used corporately concerning the church. For example, *Isaiah 2:2* declares *"that . . . in the last days the mountain of the Lord's house shall be ESTABLISHED in the top of the mountains. . ."* God's desire is to "set fast, make stable and solid", His house in the last days. In order for that to come to pass, there must be an understanding of what God is speaking into the life of the Church and the individual Christian today.

What is "present truth"? It is that portion of God's Word that the Holy Spirit is emphasizing at this time. A study of church history reveals that the great reformers, beginning approximately 500 years ago, came forth in their generations declaring truths that had been ignored or neglected. The

Holy Spirit, through these men of God, spoke concerning that which God wanted re-established in the hearts of His people. Martin Luther came with a word of "justification by faith alone". This word was "present truth" in Martin Luther's day. Later there was a "present truth" concerning water baptism. In John Wesley's day, "present truth" was holiness and sanctification. This emphasis of the Spirit in each generation is very important as God restores the Church to its former glory and power, that He might present to Himself a *"glorious church"*, without *"spot or wrinkle" (Ephesians 5:27)*.

It is our belief and conviction that God is speaking about certain areas of truth to the Church today. In this particular book, you will find a "rhema", a present word being emphasized to the Body of Christ. You will hear the truths of restoration, the principles that God uses to restore His people. You will read concerning the subjects of worship, the heart desire of God from Genesis to Revelation, the concept of the local church, the Body of Jesus Christ, and other principles that are making the Church a powerful instrument in the hand of the Lord in these last days.

It is my desire as we have brought this book together, that it will enable you to understand the Holy Spirit's emphasis in these days concerning the building up of the Body of Jesus Christ. I believe that as you give yourself to prayer and meditation, these truths will come alive in your life as they have for the past many years in the life of our church here in Portland, Oregon. May God quicken your mind as you read this textbook on PRESENT DAY TRUTHS.

Pastor K.R. (Dick) Iverson.

CHAPTER ONE

The Church As God's Holy Nation

The Church
As God's
Holy Nation
Chapter One

In this present day visitation not all that God is doing is a "new thing". We often think He is doing a "new thing" because what He is doing is new to us. What God is doing today must be seen in relation to the eternal purposes of God *(Ephesians 3:9-11)*. Before the foundations of the world were laid, God, in the very counsel of the Godhead, determined His eternal purposes; and although this plan and purpose may be a "mystery" to man, God has always been in control.

God has never been caught unawares. From the Book of Genesis (Book of Beginnings) God has declared His purpose to man. And God said, *"Let us make man* **IN OUR IMAGE,** *after our likeness: and let* **THEM** *have dominion over the fish of the sea, and over the fowl of the air, and over the cattle, and over all the earth, and over every creeping thing that creepeth upon the earth" (Genesis 1:26).* God has always desired to have a man in His image. This work was begun in Adam, but Adam didn't stand up to the tests involved. When Adam fell into sin God did not abandon His eternal purpose, but in the event of Adam's fall, He had provided a **PLAN** whereby man might be restored, and the purposes of God might be fulfilled. This Plan has never changed. The Plan set forth in the Old Testament is the same as the Plan revealed in the New Testament. All of human history can be seen as a progressive unfolding of the **PLAN** of Redemption - the Plan to create a man in the image of God.

It is in this eternal plan and purpose of God that we find the Church — God's Holy Nation. The New Testament Church, local and universal is at the very center of the plans and purposes of God. It is the New Testament Church operating as the Body of Christ that will ultimately fulfill and bring to completion all that God purposed in the beginning *(Revelation 12:5 and Revelation 21:1-4)*.

For this reason it is important for us to know what God has to tell us in regard to the nature and function of the Church. The questions contained in this chapter are aimed at giving us a scriptural picture of what the Church is.

1.   IS THE CHURCH UNIQUE TO THE NEW TESTA-MENT OR CAN IT BE FOUND IN THE OLD TESTA-MENT?

As we have stated, the Church has been part of the eternal purposes of God since the foundation of the world. All of the Old Testament points to that which is to be fulfilled in Christ and His Church. In fact, Israel is spoken of as *"The Church in the Wilderness"* *(Acts 7:38)*.

Hebrews 12:22-23 - "But ye are come unto Mount Zion, and unto the city of the living God, the heavenly Jerusalem, and unto an innumerable company of angels, to the general assembly and the Church of the first-born, which are written in heaven, and to God the Judge of all, and to the spirits of just men made perfect."

See also I Peter 2:5,9.

The writer to the Hebrews declares that Mount Zion and the Church of the Firstborn are synonymous. There can be no dispute that all of these terms speak of the church which is His Body. The New Testament writers, being the infallible interpreters of the Old Testament, tell us that the Mt. Zion of the Old Testament points to the New Testament assembly of the saints. The Mount Zion of the Old Testament points to the Church of the New Testament. What does God tell us about Zion in the Old Testament? Note the following:

Psalm 87:2-3, 5-7 — "The Lord loveth the gates of Zion more than all the dwellings of Jacob. Glorious things are spoken of thee, O city of God. . . And of Zion it shall be said, This and that man was born in her: and the highest Himself shall establish her. The Lord shall count, when he writeth up the people, that this man was born there. As well the singers as the players on instruments shall be there: all my springs are in thee."

Psalm 132:13-17 — "For the Lord hath chosen Zion: He hath desired it for His habitation. This is My rest forever: here will I dwell: for I have desired it. I will abundantly bless her provision: I will satisfy her poor with bread. I will clothe also her priests with salvation; and her saints shall shout aloud for joy. There will I make the horn of David to bud."

Isaiah 14:32 — "What shall one then answer the messengers of the nation? That the Lord hath founded Zion, and the poor of His people shall trust in it."

Isaiah 28:16 — "Therefore thus saith the Lord God, Behold, I lay in Zion for a foundation a stone, a tried stone, a precious corner stone, a sure foundation: he that believeth shall not make haste."

Micah 4:2 — "And many nations shall come, and say, Come, and let us go up to the mountain of the house of the Lord, and to the house of the God of Jacob; and He will teach us of His ways, and we will walk in His paths: for the law shall go forth of Zion, and the Word of the Lord from Jerusalem."

Zechariah 2:10-11 — "Sing and rejoice, O daughter of Zion: for, lo, I come, and I will dwell in the midst of thee, saith the Lord. And many nations shall be joined to the Lord in that day, and shall be My people: and I will dwell in the midst of thee, and thou shalt know that the Lord of hosts hath sent me unto thee."

See also Psalm 2:6; 14:7; 102:13-16; 125:1; Isaiah 2:3; 4:3-5; 40:9; 51:16; 52:1-2; Jeremiah 50:28.

The promises that God gave to Israel in the Old Testament are to flow into the Church of the New Testament, Spiritual Israel *(Galatians 6:16)*. The responsibilities given to the men of Israel in the Old Testament are to be fulfilled by the Household of Faith in the New Testament. Israel was a nation chosen by God to bless the world with the knowledge of the true God and the Messianic message. As a nation they failed to achieve this under the Law. God has called a holy nation through His Son which will indeed bless the nations (gentiles, heathen) with the message of the Gospel.

Genesis 12:2-3 — "And I will make of thee a great nation, and I will bless thee, and make thy name great; and thou shalt be a blessing: And I will bless them that bless thee, and curse them that curseth thee: and in thee shall all families of the earth be blessed."

Isaiah 2:2 — "And it shall come to pass in the last days, that the mountain of the Lord's house shall be established in the top of the mountains, and shall be exalted above the hills; and all nations shall flow unto it."

All of the Old Testament foreshadowed what was to come to us in Christ. All of the prophets spoke of Christ and His Body, the Church.

I Corinthians 10:11 — "Now all these things happened unto them for ensamples: and they are written for our admonition, upon whom the ends of the world are come."

I Peter 1:10-12 — "Of which salvation the prophets have enquired and searched diligently, who prophesied of the grace that should come unto you: searching what, or what manner of time the Spirit of Christ which as in them did signify, when it testified beforehand the sufferings of Christ, and the glory that should follow. Unto whom it was revealed, that not unto themselves, but unto us they did minister the things, which are now reported unto you by them that have preached the Gospel unto you with the Holy Ghost sent down from heaven; which things the angels desire to look into."

Romans 15:4 — "For whatsoever things were written aforetime were written for our learning, that we through patience and comfort of the scriptures might have hope."

Acts 26:22-23 — "Having therefore obtained help of God, I continue unto this day, witnessing both to small and great, saying none other things than those which the prophets and Moses did say should come: that Christ should suffer, and that He sould be the first that should rise from the dead, and should shew light unto the people, and to the Gentiles."

See also Acts 3:18-20; Matthew 5:17-18; Luke 24:27; Galatians 3:24; Hebrews 10:1,7.

2.   **WHAT DID CHRIST TELL US ABOUT THE CHURCH?**

Jesus Himself is the first one to use the word "Church". In His teaching He refers to two aspects of the Church.

Matthew 16:16-18 — "And Simon Peter answered and said, Thou are the Christ, the Son of the living God. And Jesus answered and said unto him, Blessed are thou, Simon Barjona: for flesh and blood hath not revealed it unto thee, but My Father which is in heaven. And I say also unto thee, That thou are Peter, and upon this rock I will build my **CHURCH**: *and the gates of hell shall not prevail against it."*

In the first reference to the Church, Christ points us to the invisible **CHURCH UNIVERSAL** (See Page *14*). We notice the following with regard to this statement by Jesus:

The Church is . . . . .
   a) His Church.
   b) One Church (not plural).
   c) Built by Christ Himself.
   d) Built on the Rock (spiritual locality) which is Jesus Christ.
   e) Built on the basis of a revelation of who Jesus Christ is.
   f) To be triumphant over the very gates of hell.
   g) To have authority to bind and loose on earth and in heaven *(vs. 19).*

Christ refers to the **VISIBLE** or **LOCAL CHURCH** in His second use of the word "Church".

Matthew 18:15-20 — "Moreover if thy brother shall trespass against thee, go and tell him his fault between thee and him alone: if he shall hear thee, though hast gained thy brother. But if he will not hear thee, then take with thee one or two more, that in the mouth of two or three witnesses every word may be established. And if he shall neglect to hear them, tell it to the **CHURCH**: *but if he neglect to hear the* **CHURCH**, *let him be unto thee as an heathen man and a publican. Verily I say unto you, Whatsoever ye shall bind on earth shall be bound in heaven: and whatsoever ye shall loose on earth shall be loosed in heaven. Again I say unto you, That if two of you shall agree on earth as touching any thing that they shall ask, it shall be done for them of My Father which is in heaven. For where* *two or three are gathered together in My Name, there am I in the midst of them.''*

In this brief passage Christ tells us a great deal about the visible, local Church and how it is to function. Observe the following:
The Church is . . .
   a) Composed of brothers.
   b) Involved in areas of discipline.
   c) An area of local government.
   d) A defined body from which one could be expelled.
   e) A place having power to bind and loose in heaven and on earth.
   f) A place of fellowship in faitn and prayer.
   g) A gathering identified with the **NAME** of Christ.
   h) A place where Christ promises to be in the midst.

3. **HOW DOES THE JEW OF THE OLD TESTAMENT RELATE TO THE CHURCH OF THE NEW TESTAMENT?**

In Christ there is neither Jew nor Greek. Jesus is the Lamb for the whole world who broke down the middle wall of partition. All who come to God must come the same way. The present day People of God is composed of believers who are joined together in Christ Jesus in a spiritual union. The only way for anyone to enter into the Family of God is through the new birth experience *(John 3).* Old Testament natural Israel was chosen to be the nation that would bless the nations. Though they failed as a nation, this promise was fulfilled in Christ who was of the tribe of Judah. At the Cross God inaugurated the spiritual Kingdom to which the national Kingdom was to point. This is the Kingdom of His dear Son. All who stand "in Christ" are part of this Spiritual Kingdom of God.

God gave the keys of the Kingdom to the Church

(Matthew 16:19). Peter used these keys to open the door of
faith to the Jews on the Day of Pentecost, and three thousand
Jews heard the call *(Acts 2).* Later we are told that many of
the Priests were obedient to the faith. *(Acts 6:7).* These
Jews entered into the open door by faith and became part of
the Spiritual Israel of God *(Galatians 6:16).*

Later when Peter preached in the house of Cornelius
he again used the Keys of the Kingdom to unlock the door
of faith to the Gentiles. The Gospel was preached to the
Jew first and then to the Gentile. These Gentiles also heard
the call and entered through the door of faith and became
part of the Spiritual Israel of God *(Acts 10).*

There is no distinction now in Christ. The Jew has
no corner on the Kingdom of God. Those Jews that reject
Christ are no more God's people. Those Jews that rejected
Christ were cast off from the Israel of God. Those Gentiles
that accepted Christ were grafted into the Olive Tree of
God's people. Note the following Scriptures:

*Romans 9:8 — "That is, they which are the children
of the flesh, these are not the children of God: but
the children of the promise are counted for the
seed."*

*Ephesians 2:11-21 — "Wherefore remember, that ye
being in time past Gentiles in the flesh, who are called
uncircumcision by that which is called the circumcision
in the flesh made by hands; That at that time ye were
without Christ, being aliens from the commonwealth
of Israel, and strangers from the covenants of promise,
having no hope and without God in the world: But now
in Christ Jesus ye who sometimes were far off are made
nigh by the blood of Christ. For he is our peace, who
hath made both one, and hath broken down the middle
wall of partition between us; Having abolished in his
flesh the enmity, even the law of commandments contained in ordinances; for to make in himself of twain
one new man, so making peace; And that he might*

reconcile both unto God in one body by the cross, having slain the enmity thereby: And came and preached peace to you which were afar off, and to them that were nigh. Now therefore ye are no more strangers and foreigners, but fellow-citizens with the saints, and of the household of God; And are built upon the foundation of the apostles and prophets, Jesus Christ Himself being the chief corner stone; In whom all the building fitly framed together groweth unto an holy temple in the Lord."

Acts 3:19-24 — "Repent ye therefore, and be converted, that your sins may be blotted out, when the times of refreshing shall come from the presence of the Lord; And he shall send Jesus Christ which before was preached unto you: Whom the heaven must receive unto the times of restitution of all things, which God hath spoken by the mouth of all his holy prophets since the world began. For Moses truly said unto the fathers, A prophet shall the Lord your God raise up unto you of your brethren, like unto me; him shall ye hear in all things whatsoever he shall say unto you. And it shall come to pass, that every soul, which will not hear that prophet, shall be destroyed from among the people. Yea, and all the prophets from Samuel and those that follow after, as many as have spoken, have likewise foretold of these days."

Romans 11:1-4 — "I say then, Hath God cast . . . away his people? God forbid. For I also am an Israelite, of the seed of Abraham, of the tribe of Benjamin. God hath not cast away his people which he foreknew. Wot ye not what the Scripture saith of Elias? How he maketh intercession to God against Israel, saying, Lord, they have killed thy prophets, and digged down thine altars; and I am left alone, and they seek my life. But what saith the answer of God unto him? I have reserved to myself seven thousand men, who have not bowed the knee to the image of Baal."

Romans 11:17 — "And if some of the branches be broken off, and thou, being a wild olive tree, were grafted in among them, and with them partakest of the root and fatness of the olive tree."

See also Romans 2:28-29; 3:26; and Galatians 4:22-31.

The ultimate restoration coming to the Jew is a spiritual restoration that comes to all who receive Christ. The only way that any Jew can become part of the Olive Tree again is by accepting Christ as his Messiah. When he does this he becomes a member of the Body of Christ, the Church, the Called-out Ones. (See chart on the following page).

Ephesians 1:4,10 - "According as he hath chosen us in him before the foundation of the world, that we should be holy and without blame before him in love: That in the dispensation of the fulness of times he might gather together in one all things in Christ, both which are in heaven, and which are on earth; even in him."

Ephesians 3:5-6— "Which in other ages was not made known unto the sons of men, as it is now revealed unto his holy apostles and prophets by the Spirit; That the gentiles should be fellowheirs, and of the same body, and partakers of his promise in Christ by the gospel."

Ephesians 3:10-11 — "To the intent that now unto the principalities and powers in heavenly places might be known by the church the manifold wisdom of God, according to the eternal purpose which he purposed in Christ Jesus our Lord."

See also, I Peter 1:10-12.

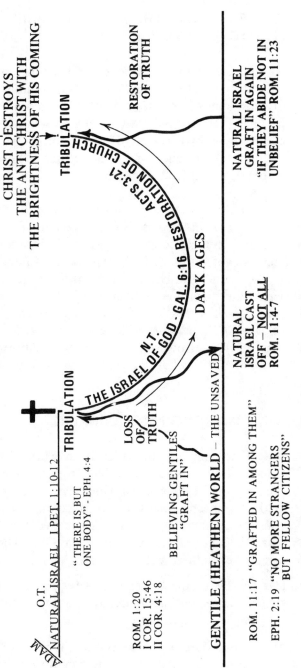

THE RAPTURE AND REVELATION OF JESUS "2ND COMING"

CHRIST DESTROYS THE ANTI CHRIST WITH THE BRIGHTNESS OF HIS COMING

TRIBULATION

RESTORATION OF TRUTH

NATURAL ISRAEL GRAFT IN AGAIN "IF THEY ABIDE NOT IN UNBELIEF" ROM. 11:23

ACTS 3:21 RESTORATION OF CHURCH

N.T. THE ISRAEL OF GOD - GAL. 6:16 RESTORATION

DARK AGES

TRIBULATION

LOSS OF TRUTH

BELIEVING GENTILES "GRAFT IN"

NATURAL ISRAEL CAST OFF – NOT ALL ROM. 11:4-7

O.T.

NATURAL ISRAEL I PET. 1:10-12

"THERE IS BUT ONE BODY" - EPH. 4:4

ROM. 1:20
I COR. 15:46
II COR. 4:18

ADAM

GENTILE (HEATHEN) WORLD – THE UNSAVED

ROM. 11:17 "GRAFTED IN AMONG THEM"

EPH. 2:19 "NO MORE STRANGERS BUT FELLOW CITIZENS"

EPH. 3:6 " GENTILES FELLOW HEIRS OF THE SAME BODY"

4.   IS THE CHURCH, THE BODY OF CHRIST, MYSTICAL OR VISIBLE?

As we have seen from Christ's own teaching, the Church is both mystical and visible. Because of the importance of this subject in the present "Visitation" of God, it is necessary for us to see what God's Word has to say about these two aspects of the Church. We want to maintain the balance of the Scriptures themselves and emphasize what God emphasizes.

Throughout the New Testament the word "Church" is used 114 times. Ninety percent of the time it refers to a visible, local congregation in a set location. To say that God is not interested in the Local Church is not putting the emphasis where God puts it. God indeed recognized the invisible or mystical Church which is made up of all believers of every age, living or dead. In fact, *"THEY without US are not made perfect" (Hebrews 11:40)*. However, it is very important that we do not belittle what God has provided in the local assembly.

5.   WHAT IS THE INVISIBLE CHURCH?

It is that company of believers in Christ in all ages, living and dead, who are distinct from the world by virtue of their calling from God. The word "Church" (Ekklesia) means "that which is called out". The Church consists of those who have been called out from the world and have been separated unto God. Therefore it cannot be confused with a reformed world.

The Epistle to the Ephesians deals primarily with the nature of the invisible Church. From it we glean the following:

a)   There is but one universal Church *(1:22)*. Many people are disturbed that they do not find everyone who is saved a part of the organization. The problem is not nearly as serious when you realize that this passage, as others like it, is discussing that which is invisible.

See also Romans 12:5; I Corinthians 10:17

b)   The Church is a living proclamation to the visible and the invisible world of the manifold wisdom of God *(3:21)*. God is not only showing His grace to man, but He is showing His wisdom to Principalities and powers. The Wisdom of God finds its supreme manifestation in His grace in the Church.

c)   The Church is something that exists throughout all ages *(3:21)*. The Church was in the eternal purposes of God. Therefore the Church cannot be a parenthesis which God arranged when the Jew rejected Christ. Had the Jew received Christ He would still have established the Church.

The purposes of God do not merely flow through the Church, as they do through the world, but they flow to the Church. God's final objective is to bring this Church to Eternal Glory. The Church will never be superseded by a Kingdom or anything else.

d)   The Church is subject to its Head, Jesus Christ *(5:24)*. God presents this subjection in the picture of the family relationship. Any subjection to any authority which is not authorized by Christ is infidelity and adultery and leads to alienation.

e)   The Church is redeemed by Christ and therefore, loved by Christ *(5:25)*. The Love of God and the Plan of Redemption are particularly and peculiarly related to the Church, even as a husband has a peculiar relation to his own wife that differs from his relationship to all other women.

f)   The Church is to be without spot or wrinkle when the Bride is presented to the Father *(5:27)*. Positionally, the invisible Church is already in this condition. As the end of all things is at hand God desires to bring our experience up to our position "in Christ".

g)   The Church is nourished and cherished by Christ. *(5:29)*. Just as the husband provides for the wife, Christ provides all that we need.

h)   The Church is one with Christ. *(5:32)*. Christ is the risen Head of the Church. Just as our natural head is one with our natural body, so is Christ (the Head) one with His Body (the Church). Just as the head contains the brains and directs the natural body, so Christ is to direct His Church.

i)   The Church can be compared to a Building or Temple of God *(2:20 - 22)*. The Church is a Temple of living stones builded by God and inhabited by God. This present Temple is built around the True Altar, sprinkled by the Blood of Christ, resting on Christ the Corner Stone, and the site of spiritual sacrifices and worship unto God. This is the Temple that God is restoring in the last days.

j)   The Church is to be the fulness of Christ *(1:23)*. The Church is to be the place where all the attributes of God are found in their proper balance. The Church is to be that visible avenue having the knowledge of the love of Christ and expressing the fulness of God to the world *(3:19)*. This is the ultimate goal of the Church to come *"unto a perfect man, unto the measure of the stature of the fulness of Christ" (4:13)*. It will take place experientially in God's *"fulness of times" (1:10)*.

k)   The Church is the Body of Christ *(1:23,* the significance of this will be discussed in a later chapter*)*.

l)   The Church is the Army of the Lord to do spiritual battle against the powers of darkness *(6:10-13)*.

The Invisible Church involves a mystical union of all believers of all ages into a spiritual body for the habitation of the Spirit with Jesus Christ as its Head. It is not a union which can presently be seen in the visible sense, but it is an invisible reality in the eyes of God.

6.   WHAT IS THE VISIBLE OR LOCAL CHURCH?

A Local Church is a New Testament organization of:
(1)   groups of believers in given localities, which are marked out by
(2)   confession of faith,
(3)   discipline of life,
(4)   obedience in baptism,
(5)   gathered to the Person of Christ,
(6)   having gifted ministries from Christ,
(7)   and keeping the memorial of the death of Jesus Christ.

They are always spoken of as:
(8)   complete units within themselves, which may,
(9)   voluntarily cooperate and fellowship with one another.

The Book of Acts gives us a developing picture of what a Local Church is to be. The Church in the Book of Acts is the Church that was instituted by Christ and is to be the pattern of all subsequent Churches. From the Book of Acts we notice that the following are characteristic of a New Testament Local Church:

The Local Church is. . . .

a) a congregation or assembly of people in a given locality *(8:1)*.
b) an assembly of believers in Christ *(5:14)*.
c) a place of teaching and discipline *(11:26)*.
d) a complete unity in itself with corporate authority *(15:22)*.
e) built by Christ Himself *(2:47)*.
f) part of Christ Himself *(5:14)*.
g) a place to which the Lord joins people, not man *(5:13)*.
h) disciplined by Christ Himself *(5:5)*.
i) structured; having men ordained in positions of authority to exercise leadership, discipline and oversight *(14:23; 20:17-28)*.
j) a place of manifold ministry *(13:1; 15:4)*.
k) joined in voluntary fellowship with other local Churches *(15:3-4)*.
l) a place established in the faith *(16:5)*.
m) a place from which ministry is sent out *(13:2)*.

Acts 2:42 - "And they continued steadfastly in the Apostles' doctrine, and fellowship, and in breaking of bread, and in prayers."

As we read through the Book of Acts we cannot help but be impressed by the importance of the Local Church to every born again believer. Being a member of a Local Church is clearly pictured as a natural result of receiving the Lord. No one who IS NOT saved has a right to be a member of a local congregation, and no one who IS saved should be without a spiritual home. Even Paul, that great missionary-Apostle maintained a firm relationship to the Local Church that had sent him out (Antioch).

Everything that is true in the absolute sense concerning the invisible Church should manifest itself in principle and in relative degrees in the Local Church. The ideal, as stated objectively in regard to the invisible Church, is the guiding principle for the local congregation.

7. **HOW DOES THE CONCEPT OF THE KINGDOM OF GOD RELATE TO THE INVISIBLE AND THE VISIBLE CHURCH?**

The Kingdom of God can be simply defined as the visible description of the body of professing Christians across the earth, or an extension of God's rule in the Universe. The preaching of the Kingdom is an important part of the vision of the Church. Jesus spoke for forty days on the things pertaining to the Kingdom of God to prepare His disciples for coming ministry. *(Acts 1:1-3).*

See also Acts 8:12; 14:22; 19:8; 20:25; 28:23; Colossians 1:13.

Psalms 145:10-13 - "All Thy works shall praise Thee, O Lord; and Thy saints shall bless Thee. They shall speak of the glory of Thy Kingdom, and talk of Thy power; to make known to the sons of men His mighty acts, and the glorious majesty of His Kingdom. Thy Kingdom is an everlasting Kingdom, and Thy dominion endureth throughout all generations."

8. **WHAT IS THE GREAT COMMISSION GIVEN TO THE CHURCH BY CHRIST?**

There can be no proper study of the churches in the

New Testament apart from an analysis of the Great Commission. The significance of the Great Commission is that it not only constitutes the most essential task of the churches, but that the churches themselves are born because of obedience by some to the Great Commission. Without the Great Commission there would not be any churches. It is to be noted that while there is in the commission that which will bring about a Local Church, there is nothing in it that indicates we are to form any kind of organized religion or organizational hierarchy, such as denominationalism.

Before Christ left earth in His final Ascension He commissioned the Church to carry on in the ministry that He began. In itself this was an impossible commission. With the commission, however, Jesus promised to send an enduement with power from on high that would enable these men to fulfill the commission. Both Matthew and Mark record the commission given to the disciples. It would do us well to examine each phrase of this commission to see what is fully involved.

THE GREAT COMMISSION - Matthew 28:18-20 and Mark 16:15-20

    a)   Jesus said, *"All power is given unto Me in heaven and in earth" (Matthew 28:18).*

When Christ commissioned his faltering and failing followers, He did it on the basis of the absolute authority available to carry out this super-human task. Nobody can begin to dent the need, nor understand the problem unless

they grasp this basis and resource in the exalted Lord. Mark gives a very practical definition of the phrases and aspects of this power and resource which is in Christ.

Christ gave power relating to:

1) The SPIRITUAL KINGDOM, for *"He that be-lieveth and is baptized shall be saved" (Mark 16:16).*

2) The ETERNAL KINGDOM, for *"He that be-lieveth not shall be damned" (Mark 16:16).*

3) The SATANIC KINGDOM, for they shall *"cast out devils" (Mark 16:17).*

4) The UNIVERSAL KINGDOM, for *"they shall speak with new tongues" (Mark 16:17).*

5) The ANIMAL KINGDOM, for *"they shall take up serpents" (Mark 16:18).*

6) The MINERAL KINGDOM, for *"if they drink any deadly thing, it shall not hurt them" (Mark 16:18).*

7) The HUMAN KINGDOM, for *"they shall lay hands on the sick, and they shall recover" (Mark 16:18).*

Mark gives us a graphic portrayal of what the "all power" in Matthew's Gospel speaks. This demonstrates for us the power that was given to Christ, which He gave to the Church to carry out His ministry in the earth. What a wealth of power God has placed in the hands of His people! Some would rob us of the power of God by asserting that this sec-tion in Mark is not part of the original manuscript, but all one has to do is turn to the Book of Acts for a dramatic por-trayal of all that is suggested in these passages of Mark.

b) Jesus said, *"Go ye therefore, and teach (disciple, matheteuo) all nations" (Matthew 28:19).*

This is the first command given to the Church. Mark

says we are to *"Go. . . into all the world and preach the Gospel to every creature" (Mark 16:15).* The thoughts contained in these verses indicate that we are to preach the Gospel with the intent of making disciples. Our function as a Church is not merely to get people saved. God is not interested in a group of frail spiritual babies, even though we all must begin there. He is not interested in a Body of Believers that spend most of their Christian life backsliding and re-dedicating themselves. He wants disciples who are willing to lay down all, take up their cross and follow Him. For this to happen we must not hide the cost of discipleship in our teaching and preaching of the Gospel, but we must give everyone the opportunity to count the cost before starting to build.

    c)   Jesus told us to baptize *"them in the NAME of the Father, and the Son, and the Holy Ghost" (Matthew 28:19).*

This is how a Local Church is founded. People in a given area who receive Christ and are identified with His Name (Lord Jesus Christ) in water baptism are joined together in their common interest. This initial act of obedience to and identification with Christ is the foundation of the Local Church. We notice that it is a command to baptize. It is not put forth as an option. All those who have truly laid down their life will want to be obedient to every command of the Gospel.

    d)   Jesus told us to teach (instruct in doctrine, didasko) *". . .them to observe all things whatsoever I have commanded you" (Matthew 28:20).*

God is not interested in just getting people saved. If all we do is evangelize the world, we have not fulfilled the Great Commission. God wants us to teach and instruct in doctrine all the nations. Why? Because He wants a glorious Church without spot or wrinkle. *(Ephesians 4:12-13).* He wants us to all come to the unity of the faith. We cannot fulfill this command with a "mission", a tract or a radio message. For this commission to be fulfilled there must be a planting of Local Churches which have taken seriously the command of Christ. There must be a place where the new plants can be nourished and watered. New born babes in Christ must have a home in which they can be fed and established in the faith *(Psalm 68:6)*.

Just as the local synagogue was a place of learning and instruction for the Jew, the Local Church is to be a place of disiplined instruction in the Word of God. The Church is to teach all things commanded by Christ. The mission of the Church goes well beyond evangelism. The Church is to teach the commands and the doctrines of Christ.

  e) Jesus said, *"Lo, I am with you alway, even unto the end of the world" (Matthew 28:20)*.

Apart from this we have no chance of fulfilling what Jesus has commanded. As we stand "in Christ" we are able to boldly say with Paul, *"The Lord is my Helper, and I will not fear what man shall do unto me" (Hebrews 13:6)*. It is the Presence of Christ "in the midst" that makes the Church a place of power and authority *(Matthew 18:20)*. He has promised to be present with power in the midst of a praising people *(Psalm 22:3)* to attend the ministry and to manifest supernatural confirmation of the Gospel *(Mark 16:20)*. It is the Presence of the Lord that gives power to the Gospel. The power of His Presence is promised unto the END OF THE WORLD! This means that this power is for us as well as for the early Church. What effect can the Church of today have if it is not empowered by the Presence of the Lord? We must go as the disciples did or go not at all. As the disciples received the command and went forth the Lord was working in them, *"confirming the Word with signs following" (Mark 16:20)*.

  f) Jesus was *"received up into heaven, and sat on the right hand of God" (Mark 16:19)*.

Jesus takes His place as the Risen Head of the Church which is His Body. As He ascended and was exalted He was able to send the promise of the Father, the Holy Spirit to direct and administrate the Churches which were created by the proclamation of the Great Commission. Christ is the Head and the ultimate authority in the Body of Christ. Nowhere is this authority given to any man, any counsel or any organization of men. The authority is given to the place where Christ is present *(Matthew 18:20)*. It is given to the Local Church and is committed to faithful men in local congregations who maintain a direct contact with the Holy Spirit and will give account directly to the Lord Jesus and not to some ecclesiastical authority (See chapter on Church Order).

The commission which Christ gave to the Church is to be seen in relation to each individual believer. It is completely established by the pattern of the New Testament practice that this commission was not limited to the Apostles, ordained ministry or to any segment of Christians, but it extends to each and every believer in Jesus Christ. The Great Commission is the command of the risen Lord to His disciples wherever they may be found. Every person who professes faith in Christ must answer before God concerning his or her obedience to Christ's command.

9. **WHY ARE THERE SO MANY NAMES GIVEN TO THE CHURCH, THE PEOPLE OF GOD?**

There are more than seventy names given to the people of God in both the Old and New Testaments. The names given to the people of God in the Old Testament are to be applied to the Church of the New Testament. The Old Testament was written for our admonition *(I Corinthians 10:11)*. Therefore when Israel is mentioned in the Old Testament it was written for the Church, to teach the Church the ways and dealings of God. The TRUE Israel in God's eyes is Spiritual Israel which is made up of both Jews and Gentiles, *"That is, they which are the children of the flesh, these are not the children of God: but the children of the promise are counted for the seed" (Romans 9:8).* Therefore all of the names that describe God's people in the Old Testament can be rightfully applied to the Body of Christ. *(Romans 11:1-5, 17).*

As we have said, the Church was conceived in the counsels of the Godhead. It is part and parcel of the very purposes of God. For this reason it is a "mystery" in the sense that finite man may never fully understand all that is involved in this Body and its relation to Christ. God has given us over seventy names and descriptions of the people of God to show us the many facets and aspects of truth concerning this infinite reality. Each name adds to the total concept and unfolds another facet of truth in regard to God's people.

10. **WHAT ARE SOME OF THE NAMES GIVEN TO THE PEOPLE OF GOD?**

a) His Body - Christ is the Head of the Church. As the Head is the seat of authority which commands the rest of the Body, so Christ is the Head of the Church. As the head gives direction and the body obeys and carries out the desires of the head, even so does Christ direct His Church.

Ephesians 1:22-23 - "And hath put all things under his feet and gave him to be the head over all things to the church, which is his body, the fulness of him that filleth all in all."

b) Holy Temple - Christ is the Masterbuilder who is building a Temple for His permanent habitation.

Ephesians 2:21 - "In whom all the building fitly framed together groweth unto an holy temple in the Lord."

c) Habitation of God - It has ever been God's desire to

dwell with and in His people *(Exodus 25:8; Psalm 22:3).*

Ephesians 2:22 - "In whom ye also are builded together for an habitation of God through the Spirit."

d) God's Building - The Church has its origin in God. It is not built by man.

I Corinthians 3:9 - "For we are labourers together with God: ye are God's husbandry, ye are God's building."

e) God's House - God is the Lord of this home and is to be the one in charge.

Hebrews 3:6 - "But Christ as a son over his own house; whose house are we, if we hold fast the confidence and the rejoicing of the hope firm unto the end."

f) Spiritual House - This house is not made with ordinary building materials but it is a spiritual structure held together by the bonds of love.

I Peter 2:6 - "Ye also, as lively stones, are built up a spiritual house, an holy priesthood, to offer up spiritual sacrifices, acceptable to God by Jesus Christ."

g) Holy Nation - This is to be a group or nation of people that are set apart to do the will of God.

I Peter 2:9 - "But ye are a chosen generation, a royal priesthood, an holy nation, a peculiar people; that ye should shew forth the praises of him who hath called you out of darkness into his marvellous light."

h) People of God - These people recognize that they were bought with a price, and they are not their own.

I Peter 2:10 - "Which in time past were not a people, but are now the people of God: which had not obtained mercy, but now have obtained mercy."

i) Israel of God - This is God's chosen nation. He has set this people aside to be a peculiar people in the earth.

Galatians 6:14-16 - "But God forbid that I should glory, save in the cross of our Lord Jesus Christ, by whom the world is crucified unto me, and I unto the world. For in Christ Jesus neither circumcision availeth anything, nor uncircumcision, but a new creature. And as many as walk according to this rule, peace be on them, and mercy, and upon the Israel of God."

j) Mt. Zion - This is the Mountain that God raised and upon which He places His glory.

Hebrews 12:22 - "But ye are come unto Mount Zion, and unto the city of the living God, the heavenly Jerusalem, and to an innumerable company of angels."

k) Heavenly Jerusalem - The Church is the spiritual city to which earthly Jerusalem pointed.

Hebrews 12:22 - "But ye are come unto Mount Zion, and unto the city of the living God, the heavenly Jerusalem, and to an innumerable company of angels."

l) General Assembly - This is an innumerable company from every nation, kindred, tongue and tribe who have gathered themselves unto the Lord Jesus Christ.

Hebrews 12:23 - "To the general assembly and church of the firstborn, which are written in heaven, and to God the Judge of all, and to the spirits of just men made perfect."

m) Church of the Firstborn - This is the group that
    "in Christ" can lay hold of a double portion of the
    blessings of God.

*Hebrews 12:23 - "To the general assembly and church of
the firstborn, which are written in heaven, and to God
the Judge of all, and to the spirits of just men made
perfect."*

n) Wife - There is a rich future for the wife of the King.

*Revelation 19:7 - "Let us be glad and rejoice and give
honour to him: for the marriage of the Lamb is come,
and his wife hath made herself ready."*

*Ephesians 5:25-32 - "Husbands, love your wives, even as
Christ also loved the church, and gave himself for it; That
he might sanctify and cleanse it with the washing of
water by the word, That he might present it to himself a
glorious church, not having spot, or wrinkle, or any such
thing; but that it should be holy and without blemish.
So ought men to love their wives as their own bodies.
He that loveth his wife loveth himself. For no man ever
yet hated his own flesh; but nourisheth and cherisheth it,
even as the Lord the church: For we are members of his
body, of his flesh, and of his bones. For this cause shall
a man leave his father and mother, and shall be joined
unto his wife, and they two shall be one flesh. This is a
great mystery: but I speak concerning Christ and the
church."*

There are many other names for the Body of Christ. This is
a vast subject for which we can only give an introduction. For
further study in this area refer to Nave's Topical Bible.

STUDY QUESTIONS FOR CHAPTER ONE

1. Where is the Church found in the Old Testament?

2. What is the significance of *I Corinthians 10:11?*

3. How many times did Christ refer to the Church?

4. What seven things does *Matthew 16:16-18* tell us about the universal Church?

5. What eight things does *Matthew 18:15-20* tell us about the local Church?

6. What is the only hope for the Jew?

7. Define the invisible Church.

8. Give a nine-fold definition of the visible Church.

9. What Kingdoms are believers in Christ given power over?

10. List ten names given to the people of God and the significance of each.

CHAPTER TWO

The Church From Its Power To Its Decline

The Church
From Its Power
To Its Decline

Chapter Two

We have seen a glimpse of what the Church that Christ commissioned was to be like. It was to have power over all the kingdoms of Satan and of this world. The Book of Acts demonstrate the way in which the Early Church responded to the commands of Christ. The Disciples remained in Jerusalem and waited for the promise of the Father, the out-pouring of the Holy Spirit, as Jesus had commanded. They were undoubtedly shaken up by the prospect of having to be witnesses to the same crowd that had crucified Christ. They probably questioned some of the things that Jesus said they would do in His Name. Yet, if they had learned nothing else, they had learned to be obedient to Jesus, for His Words were SPIRIT and LIFE *(John 6:63)*.

The Disciples of Christ were an unlikely group of men for such a high calling. They had been full of doubts, and at times they had to be rebuked by the Lord for their lack of faith *(Luke 8:22-25)*. They were ready to call fire down from heaven on all who rejected them *(Luke 9:54)*. Peter had been used as an instrument or mouthpiece for Satan *(Matthew 16:22-23)*. There was not one theologian among them. They were all commoners. They all had weakened in times of pressure. In fact, they had all fled when Jesus was taken captive *(Mark 14:50)*. Was this the group that Christ was addressing in *Mark 16* with the commission of the Church? Were these to be the pillars of the Early Church *(Galatians 2:9)?* In order for this to happen, the Disciples themselves were going to have to experience a real enduement of Divine power.

They were going to have to be empowered from on high.

This is the reason that Jesus told them to wait in Jerusalem until they be empowered from on high. This they did, dwelling together in one accord, in one place, in an attitude of prayer.

Acts 2:1-4 - "And when the day of Pentecost was fully come, they were all with one accord in one place. And suddenly there came a sound from heaven as of a rushing mighty wind, and it filled all the house where they were sitting. And there appeared unto them cloven tongues like as of fire, and it sat upon each of them. And they were all filled with the Holy Ghost, and began to speak with other tongues as the Spirit gave them utterance."

This baptism with the Holy Ghost *(Acts 1:5)* was the experience that transformed this shaky group of Disciples into the dynamic Apostles that Christ was to use to establish His Church. These Spirit-baptized believers were going to shake the world for God. The Church began with great power. It manifested all of the things that Christ had said it would. It was a dynamic witnessing community of believers who influenced the world with the Gospel of Christ.

11. DID THE EARLY CHURCH DEMONSTRATE OR FULFILL THE COMMISSION OF CHRIST?

The Book of Acts demonstrates that the Early Church testified to the Lord in great power, and confirmed their word with signs following. They demonstrated their power over –

a)   The SPIRITUAL KINGDOM, for through their ministry many came to know the Lord as their Saviour *(Acts 2:40-41)*.

b)   The ETERNAL KINGDOM, for those that received
      not the Apostles, received not Christ *(Matthew
      10:40).*
c)   The SATANIC KINGDOM, for demons had to flee
      at their command *(Acts 8:7; 19:12-13).*
d)   The UNIVERSAL KINGDOM, for they spake with
      other tongues as the Spirit gave them utterance
      (Acts 2:4; 10:46; 19:6).
e)   The ANIMAL KINGDOM for the venomous viper
      could not hurt the man of God *(Acts 28:3-5).*
f)   The MINERAL KINGDOM, for the poison emitted
      into Paul's body had no effect *(Acts 28:3-5).*
g)   The HUMAN KINGDOM, for they laid their hands
      on the sick, and they recovered *(Acts 28:8).*

The Church of the Book of Acts had all truth operating
in a measure. They experienced --

a)   Salvation by faith *(Acts 16:30-31).*
b)   Water baptism by immersion *(Acts 8:38,39).*
c)   Holiness and separation as Paul preached it to
      the Corinthians *(II Corinthians 6:17).*
d)   Healing practiced throughout the New Testament
      Church *(Acts 5:16).*
e)   Baptism of the Holy Ghost *(Acts 2:4).*
f)   Laying on of hands and prophecy *(Acts 13:3).*
g)   Resurrection of the dead *(Acts 9:36-40).*
h)   Eternal judgment *(Acts 5:1-11).*
i)   Praise *(Acts 16:25).*
j)   Joy *(Acts 13:52 and Romans 14:17).*

Because the Early Church literally believed, preached and
practised the whole council and Word of God, they were met
with great opposition and persecution from the kingdom of
darkness. Persecution has only ever had one effect on the true
Church of God. Persecution succeeded in scattering the
Church *(Acts 8:4),* in increasing the Church *(Acts 5:14),*
and in increasing their joy *(Acts 5:41).*

12. HOW DID THE ESTABLISHED CHURCH FAIL?

One looks at the condition of the Church in the Middle Ages and naturally asks, "How could the people be so blinded to the truth? How could they believe that what they were practising was true Christianity?" We must remember that in the time between the death of the Apostles and the Dark Ages the changes that took place were subtle and gradual. Possibly the chief cause of decline in the Church was its mixture with the things and practices of pagan religions and the world which became progressively manifest. Because of the total commitment and persecution witnessed in the Early Church, believers were forced to cling to the Lord and the communion of the saints. There was no place for the believer in the world. People who became Christians adopted an entirely different life style from their past life. They were indeed the CALLED OUT ONES.

As the Church began to become somewhat popular, its stress on a total commitment began to ebb. It began to de-emphasize the life of total separation from the things of the world, and it began to harbor mixture and impurity within its own ranks. This mixture with the world and this compromise with worldly persuasions became the leaven that eventually leavened the whole lump.

We offer the following summary of the decline of the Church:

a) 30-100A.D. - From the day of Pentecost to the death of John, the Church was a powerful instrument for the extension of the Kingdom of God. From the death of the last of the original twelve Apostles we have no evidence that this type of APOSTOLIC MINISTRY continued.

b) 130 A.D. - Because the Apostolic ministry was no longer functioning in the Early Church, the parallel ministry of the PROPHET soon vanished. With the loss of this ministry the doctrine of the LAYING ON OF HANDS became nothing more than ritual. By 140 A.D. prophetic utterance of any kind in the local congregation was very scarce.

c) 150 A.D. - With such lack of dependence on the Spirit of God and an actual persecution of the biblical manifestations of the Spirit by the established churches, it is not surprising that the biblical experience of the BAPTISM OF THE SPIRIT and the GIFTS OF THE SPIRIT were no longer evidenced by 150 A.D. Much of the external form of these things was maintained, but the people had no living encounter with the Spirit.

d) 160 A.D. - As men no longer demonstrated a Spirit-controlled life, it became impractical to have a PLURALITY OF ELDERSHIP. Without a strong unity of the Spirit multiple leadership tends to pull against another. As a result, monarchial bishops became the norm by 160 A.D., and men began to appraise clergy on the basis of natural ability.

e) 180 A.D. - If man is not able to look to the Spirit for direction and guidance, he must look to other men. And so it was with the smaller and more recently established Local Churches by 180 A.D. Many of these smaller Churches became so dependent on larger Churches that they lost their LOCAL CHURCH AUTONOMY. By this time many such churches were looking to Rome for direction, and thus, early seeds of Roman primacy are developing by this early date.

f) 200 A.D. - By this time the Spirit had very little control over the lives of individuals. Very little of the

body of Church doctrine and truth became the
actual experience of believers. A gap began to form
between doctrine and experience. The external form
remained the same in many cases, but the spiritual
awareness of what was contained in the form was
beginning to vanish. It was about this time that
Baptism began to be abused in many ways. In 185
A.D. we have the first record of an infant baptism,
and by 200 A.D. most of the Churches no longer
used the NAME of the Father, Son and Holy Spirit,
the LORD JESUS CHRIST in connection with
WATER BAPTISM as the Early Church had done.
Now they only repeated Christ's command. In
fact, it was to be later in this century that Pope
Stephen declared baptism into the Name of the
Lord Jesus Christ to be invalid.

g)   210 A.D. - Since the distinction between the clergy
and the laity was so acute by this time, the concept
of the PRIESTHOOD OF ALL BELIEVERS was
not understood or acknowledged. Therefore, the
ministry of the body of Christ (Body-ministry)
was not at all understood. Because of these trends,
the truth was soon altered to line up with experience and the ministers or clergy were the only ones
designated "priests".

h)   225 A.D. - Most Churches by this time were not
receiving direct guidance and teaching from the
Spirit of God. They could, therefore, no longer
trust the Spirit to bring and maintain unity of the
faith. In order to enforce and maintain an external
unity CREEDS or statements of beliefs began to
be written as criterion for Church membership.

i)   240 A.D. - By the middle of the third century much
worldliness had crept into the Church. Without the

power of the Spirit to lead a separate life, the standard of HOLINESS and the sanctified life held up by the Early Church became an unrealistic life for many. Some recognized this problem and began the first monasteries at this time. This made provision for a double standard in Christian living. There was the "average Christian" and the ascetic who tried to lead the "deeper life".

j) 300 A.D. - Because of the rigor of these ascetic groups, there developed an over emphasis on works as a sort of merit for eternal life. This merely laid the ground work for what was to come later under Constantine.

k) 313 A.D. - Constantine became ruler of the great Roman Empire and chose Christianity as the best possible of religions. At this time the state began to exercise control over the affairs of the established Church, and men of little or no religious experience became instrumental in shaping Church doctrine. Even the outcome of the Council of Nicea was the result of the efforts of Constantine.

l) 350 A.D. - About 350 A.D., Christianity being the religion of the state, all those who were not in the Church were persecuted. As can well be expected, many heathens preferred to be called 'Christian' rather than face the sword. At this time the experience of SALVATION with the doctrine of JUSTIFICATION BY FAITH and the new birth into the Kingdom of God was no longer emphasized.

m) 380 A.D. - This movement culminated with Theodosius who made Rome, which had already been the capital of the empire, the final authority in Church matters as well.

n)   392 A.D. - Theodosius went even further when he
     outlawed heathen worship. It now came under pen-
     alty of death for any one to have any religious
     connection other than that of the established Ro-
     man church. Those considered heathen as well as
     those considered to be heretical in their doctrine
     were openly persecuted. What a turn of events!
     The Church that had begun by being persecuted by
     the world (as Jesus predicted) now became the per-
     secutor of the heathen. This was no longer the
     Church that Christ had commissioned to preach the
     Gospel to every creature.

o)   400 A.D. - By 400 A.D. even the rite of baptism
     (for by this time that is all baptism was) was con-
     sidered unnecessary and unimportant. Many put it
     off until their death bed, while others never exper-
     ienced it at all. To a Church that was itself compris-
     ed of mostly heathen, baptism had little signifi-
     cance.

p)   484 A.D. - The cap stone to the whole Babylonish
     system came in 484 A.D. Because the emperor had
     given tax exemption to the clergy, and yet not
     willing to lose great sums of state revenue, the
     priesthood or clergy were recruited from the poorest
     and least educated classes of people. With this de-
     velopment, the Jereboam system was complete.

*I Kings 12:31 - "And he made a house of high places,
and made priests of the lowest of the people, which were
not of the sons of Levi."*

The Church in the Middle or Dark Ages was built on this
foundation. It is not hard to see why it fell to the place that
it did. It is not hard to see why the Crusades or the Inquisition
could fill the pages of Church History. Because this was no
longer the Church of our Lord, the Body of Christ. It was a

false religious system taking the Name of Christ. From this point on, the road away from God grew steeper and the compromise with the world grew greater. Due to so many unregenerated members in the Church, forms were substituted for the freedom that was once enjoyed in the Spirit of the Living God. Because of the pagan infiltration into the Church more and more compromises were made to make their stay in the Church more comfortable. The following are just a few of the areas touched by this tremendous spirit of compromise:

a) Liturgies and forms of prayers were produced (unsaved people who knew not God, naturally knew not how to pray to Him. Therefore, they needed forms to follow).

b) Church buildings became larger and more decorative. Church walls were covered with tapestries and paintings. Impressive spires adopted from heathen temples to the sun became characteristic ornamentation. Dignity and impressiveness were brought into the services. All this was to impress the natural man instead of to please God.

c) Heathen, who were accustomed to worship gods or sacred places, quickly switched over to the worship of the "saints" or first apostles, and particularly worship of Mary.

d) It was natural that the unconverted pagans now in the church would still seek material objects to worship, especially connected with places or property of the early saints. Images of the saints, pictures and the crucifix all served as objects of their worship.

e) The pagans could not trust in a God they did not KNOW: therefore they grew to trust in the bishops --those whom they could see, touch, and hear with the natural ear. Their word gradually became law, until there was no TRUTH left in the church.

f)   Because the people had been accustomed to author-
       ity coming out of Rome, the capital of the empire,
       it was a natural thing for Rome to be viewed by
       some as the seat of all authority. Gradually the Ro-
       man Church began to claim primacy in religious
       matters as the Roman state has primacy in politi-
       cal affairs. As time progressed, Rome looked for
       things that would substantiate their claim to prim-
       acy. They claimed Peter to be their first pope, even
       though present evidence suggests that Peter was
       never in Rome. This claim to authority was then
       passed down from pope to pope unto the present
       day.

13. DID GOD FORGET HIS PEOPLE?

As with Israel of old, God never let the light of truth go
out *(I Samuel 3:3)*. Throughout all of the Old Testament
history and all the apostacy of the Children of Israel,
in His infinite mercy preserved a remnant of people who
clung to the truth. God will never leave Himself without a
witness in the earth. There has been a line of faith righteous men preserved throughout the entire history of man
right up to the present day.

*II Kings 19:30-31 - "And the remnant that is escaped
out of the house of Judah shall yet again take root down-
ward, and bear fruit upward. For out of Jerusalem shall
go forth a remnant, and they that escape out of Mount
Zion: the zeal of the Lord of hosts shall do this."*

*Isaiah 1:9 - "Except the Lord of hosts had left unto us
a very small remnant, we should have been as Sodom, and
we should have been like unto Gomorrah."*

Ezekiel 14:22 - "Yet, behold, therein shall be left a remnant that shall be brought forth, both sons and daughters: behold, they shall come forth unto you, and ye shall see their way and their doings: and ye shall be comforted concerning the evil that I have brought upon Jerusalem, even concerning all that I have brought upon it."

Romans 11:5 - "Even so then at this present time also there is a remnant according to the election of grace."

See also Ezekiel 6:8; Joel 2:32; Amos 5:15; Micah 4:7; Zechariah 8:12; and Romas 9:27.

14. WHERE ARE THE TRUE PEOPLE OF GOD TO BE FOUND IN CHURCH HISTORY?

It is unfortunate, but from the middle or late second century one must look at those groups which the Church deemed heretical to find true believers worshiping God in Spirit and in turth. It is an exhaustive and tedious study, but it can be shown that God has indeed preserved a people for His Name all throughtout history. There have always been isolated groups or pockets of believers who had actually experienced the Lord and lived accordingly. From the Montanist movement through to the outbreak of the Reformation, God has had a people who were willing to serve Him whatever the cost.

STUDY QUESTIONS FOR CHAPTER TWO

1.   What level of spiritual authority was demonstrated by the Early Church?

2.   What was the primary cause of the decline of the Church?

3.   What important Bible truths were lost in the first 500 years of Church history?

4.   What was the spiritual condition of the Church in the Middle Ages?

CHAPTER THREE

God's Promise To Restore

God's Promise
To Restore

Chapter Three

The Dark Ages left the Church spiritually deaf and blind. The Church had lost its touch with the Spirit of God. As a result God's Spirit no longer led and directed this organization of man into all truth. The religious leaders of this religious system were spiritually blind, and having eyes they could not see. This Church did not listen for the voice of the Spirit behind them directing their paths, but their ears were stopped by human traditions; having ears they did not hear. The pity of it is that all the time the religious leaders and most of the people felt that they did see and did hear. They felt they were in the perfect way.

The people of the Middle Ages were duped by the traditions of men. They were a people robbed and spoiled of their spiritual heritage in Christ. They were snared by doctrines of men that made false demands upon them. They were literally bound in chains of bondage to a Babylonian system. Yet they knew it not. They had lost their deliverer (Christ) and their one hope, but because of their ignorance none said, "Restore!"

Isaiah 42:18-22 - "Hear, ye deaf; and look, ye blind, that ye may see. Who is blind, but my servant? or deaf, as my messenger that I sent? Who is blind as he that is perfect, and blind as the Lord's servant? Seeing many things, but thou observest not; opening the ears, but he heareth not. The Lord is well pleased for His righteousness' sake: He will magnify the law, and make it honorable. But this is a people robbed and spoiled; they are all of them snared

*in holes, and they are hid in prison houses: they are for
a prey, and none delivereth; for a spoil, and none saith,
Restore."*

But God is a God of faithfulness. God promised that He
would restore the people of God. It is in this chapter that we
would like to consider God's promise to restore His people
and to set their feet on higher ground.

*Acts 3:21 - "Whom the heaven must receive until the
times of restitution of all things, which God hath spoken
by the mouth of all His holy prophets since the world
began."*

15. WHAT IS A DEFINITION OF THE TERM "RESTORATION" OR "RESTITUTION"?

In the New Testament the noun form of the Greek
verb "apokathistemi" (to restore) is used only once in
Acts 3:21. The word literally means to set something
back again into its original order. This word was used in
the secular Greek world to indicate the return of a po-
ssession or a piece of land to the rightful owner. The
verb form of this word is found several times in the New
Testament. It is most often used in connection with the
miracles of Jesus who healed various conditions. In these
cases the bodies of those healed were restored to their
original state. *(See: Mark 3:5; 8:25; Matthew 12:13;
Luke 6:10).*

The Hebrew words used throughout the Old Testament
carry some of the following connotations: to be completed, to
finish, to make prosper, to recompense, to rescue, to refresh,
to set again, to retrieve, to cause to return or to renew. Restoration refers to the putting back into existence or use that
which has been lost, misplaced, or stolen.

16. WHAT IS THE SPIRITUAL SIGNIFICANCE OF "RESTORATION" IN RELATION TO THE CHURCH?

Because of the vastness of the definition of the word "restoration", it is clear that restoration involves many aspects in relation to the dealing of God with man. We saw that restoration means to "finish" or "complete". This aspect of restoration has to do with the whole of redemptive history. Ever since the fall of man into sin, God has had a plan of restoration to restore man to the place where he can ultimately experience all that God has planned in the beginning. But the thought of restoration has a particular significance in relation to the Church, for it is by the Church that the manifold wisdom of God is shown forth. Restoration for the Church involves at least three aspects:

a) Restoration involves the recovery of the Divine principles and truths that were known, believed, taught and experienced by the early Church. This would involve the recovery of those elements that were lost to the Church by the compromises made in the years of Church history. This aspect of restoration involves a returning to the foundation which was laid by the early apostles and prophets. *(See: Ephesians 2:20; I Corinthians 3:10; I Timothy 4:6).*

b) Restoration involves a renewal of spiritual life that is the result of the application of the above principles *(I Timothy 4:15-16).* As the Church returns to the pattern that God has set for it, it can not help but experience that "breath of life" that God breathed into it on the day of Pentecost. The Breath or Spirit of God brings with it that freshness and vitality that the Church of the former rain experienced.

c)   Restoration also involves a completion of God's
      plan of the ages. It involves the bringing into exis-
      tence of those things which were foretold by the
      prophets *(Acts 3:21; Romans 16:26)*. All that God
      has said, He will do. This, too, involves restoration–
      a restoration that ends up at the Tree of Life *(I
      Corinthians 15:26)*.

17. WHAT BIBLICAL TERMINOLOGY IS USED IN CONNECTION WITH THIS THEME OF RESTORATION?

As we have said, the subject of restoration is woven all
throughout the Scripture. For the student who desires to
search out this subject in a more complete way, there
are certain key phrases that are repeated often in the
Scripture that are characteristic of this subject. Some of
these phrases include the following:

a)   *"The times of restitution of all things" (Acts 3:20-
      21).*
b)   *"Return of the captivity" (Jeremiah 33:7, 11, 26;
      29:14; 30:3; Psalm 126:1; Zephaniah 3:20; Joel
      3:1; Amos 9:14-15).*
c)   *"As at the first" (Jeremiah 33:7,11; Isaiah 1:26).*
d)   *"Last days" (Joel 2:28-32).*
e)   *"Last time" (I John 2:18; Jude 18).*
f)   *"Last times" (I Peter 1:20).*
g)   *"Time of the end" (Daniel 8:17; 12:9).*
h)   *"Coming of the Lord" (I Thessalonians 5:23; 4:15).*
i)   *"Day of the Lord's anger"* or *"The day of the Lord"
      (Zephaniah 1:7,14-18; 2:2-3; I Thesslonians 5:2;
      II Peter 3:10).*
j)   *"Great and dreadful day of the Lord" (Malachi 4:5).*
k)   *"The day of vengeance of our God" (Isaiah 61:2;
      Luke 21:22).*
l)   *"Times of the Gentiles be fulfilled" (Luke 21:24;
      Romans 11:25).*
m)   *"The latter rain" (Joel 2:23-29; Hosea 6:1-2).*

18. **WHERE DOES THE SCRIPTURE DEAL WITH THE SUBJECT OF RESTORATION?**

From cover to cover, the Bible is primarily a book of RESTORATION. In the Book of Genesis, the Book of Beginnings, we have the origin of all things. Genesis is the seed-plot of the Bible. This book declares the purpose of God *(Genesis 1:26)* and the seed for every major Bible Doctrine. Everything that begins in Genesis ends up in the Book of Revelation. Revelation is a Book of Ultimates which tells us the final state of all things. The Bible gives us the history of redemption. In Genesis we are told how man lost the image of God when he fell into sin and corrupted his way. We are told how man forfeited the Tree of Life and was expelled from the Garden. We are told how God sought to restore man and provide a covering by which he might again commune with God. In Revelation we see the work of redemption completed. We see man restored to the Tree of Life. Between *Genesis 3:24 and Revelation 21:3-4* we see the panorama of restoration in its fullest sense *(See: Luke 15)*. On this basis we can expect to find this subject all throughout the Old and New Testament.

a) Restoration was the theme of the Old Testament Prophets. The prophets were divinely inspired to warn God's people of their backsliding ways and idolatry. By proclaiming God's message, the prophet endeavored to awaken the conscience of the people and to RESTORE them to righteousness and divine fellowship *(Amos 5:14)*.

1) The Book of Joel is dedicated to the theme of restoration and shows how a backslidden nation brought God's judgment upon their heads. Then, through repentance, they gained right standing, and God promised that He would "restore" *(Joel 2:18-32)*.

2)   Elijah is the classic example of a prophet who
      battled wickedness and idolatry. In *I Kings 18:
      21* he forces a decision of the people. In his
      prayer *(verse 37)* he employs an expression
      referring to restoration. It should be noted
      that it is Elijah's ministry that is often con-
      nected with that which is to take place in the
      last days *(Malachi 4:5-6; Luke 1:17; Mark 9:
      12; Matthew 17:11)*.

3)   Ezekiel depicts the message of restoration in
      fascinating visions *(Chapter 33-48)*. The
      resurrection (restoration) of the dry bones in
      chapter 37 pictures the theme of restoration
      in a most unforgetable manner.

4)   Other references include: *Psalms 23:3; 51:12;
      69:4; Isaiah 1:26; 49:6; 57:15, 18-19; 58:12;
      61:4-11; Jeremiah 30:17; Haggai 2:9*.

b)   The New Testament also emphasizes the theme of
      restoration. It would do well for us to examine what
      we are told in *Acts 3:21* which says, *"Whom the
      heavens must receive until the times of restitution
      of all things, which God hath spoken by the mouth
      of his holy prophets since the world began."*

1)   We notice that there are *"times of restitution".*
      God is working on a timetable and has every-
      thing under control. These are times when God
      will give to the Church that which was lost.
      The language here seems to imply that this
      time will immediately precede the Second
      Coming of Christ.

2)   We notice that this verse doesn't tell us that all things are going to be restored. It goes on to qualify the *"all things"* to include only those things which are spoken of by the prophets. Whatever God's holy prophets have spoken will come to pass. This is one of the tests for a true prophet. The Church should be eagerly searching the prophetic Scriptures for clues to our position in God's timetable.

3)   We notice also that Christ cannot return until all that the prophets spoke be fulfilled. Many people think that Christ could come at any minute. He could come for them any minute, but He will not come for the Church until all be fulfilled. In fact, the heavens MUST retain Him against that time, for when He returns He is coming for a fully restored Church – a Church that is glorious, not having spot or wrinkle or any such thing *(Ephesians 5:27)*.

19. WHAT ARE SOME OBVIOUS SIGNS BY WHICH WE MAY RECOGNIZE THE RESTORATION PERIOD?

All through the Scripture God has given us glimpses of what this period of time will be like. It will indeed be a glorious time of expectation and excitement, but let us look at some of the language the Bible uses of this time.

a)   The voice of joy and the voice of gladness will be heard in the House of the Lord *(Jeremiah 33:11)*. In the period of the Dark Ages the Church was in a state of mourning. The music that comes to us from that age has a mournful sound. But God is restoring His House. The present songs of Zion are songs characterized by joy, gladness, shouting and victory.

b)   The voice of the Bride will again be heard *(Jeremiah 33:11)*. The Church is to be God's mouthpiece to the world. For so many years the Church has let the world toss it to and fro. But once again the Church is arising and prophecying the Word of the Lord to the lost world. The law is going forth out of Zion.

c)   The voice of the Bridegroom will be heard among God's people *(Jeremiah 33:11)*. The Church lost that personal communion with the living Saviour when they stopped their ears to the voice of the Spirit. But Christ is coming a second time to the Church and the voice of prophecy is being heard today as never before *(Revelation 19:10)*.

d)   The voice of them that shall say "Praise the Lord" is another characteristic of restoration *(Jeremiah 33: 11)*. Over the years the Church lost the spirit of praise. They had to write down their liturgy because the song of praise was gone from their hearts. But God is raising up a generation that has a song of praise in their hearts, and it is finding expression on their lips *(Psalm 102:13-18)*.

e)   Restoration involves the return of ministries that will bring back the sacrifice of praise to the Church. *(Jeremiah 33:11)*. God is in the process of raising ministries that are leading the Church to a renewed understanding of spiritual worship. Worship is not to be a mere form, but it is to be in spirit and in truth.

f)   Restoration will also involve the return of true judges, counsellors and teachers to the church *(Isaiah 1:26; 30:8, 19-21)*. For many years the Church was run by hirelings who cared not for the flock but only the political position. In this day God

is raising up men who love the Lord, have a knowledge of His Word, are in tune with the Holy Spirit
and are motivated by a genuine desire to serve the
people of God.

g)   We can expect restoration to be a growing from
faith to faith and glory to glory *(Romans 1:17;
II Corinthians 3:17-18).* God works in response to
faith. Days of tremendous power must be days of
tremendous faith. God's method of growth is line
upon line, here a little and there a little *(Isaiah
28:10).* As the present Church is obedient to the
Word of the Lord we can expect that God will
increase our faith.

h)   As the Church is being restored we can expect that
the powers of darkness will become more pronounced. Satan doesn't have to do much against a weak
and powerless Church. But when the Church becomes strong, and he sees it as a real threat to his
Kingdom, he must work overtime. Therefore we can
expect an overt manifestation of the anti-christal
system in these days *(Revelation 13:1-8).*

i)   Restoration also has something to do with national
Israel. Although ultimate restoration for the Jew
will come only as he receives Christ *(Romans 11),*
we have to believe that Israel itself is a sign post in
God's calendar of end time events *(Isaiah 11:12;
Ezekiel 11:17; 28:25; 36:24; Amos 9:14-15; Luke
21:24).*

j)   Restoration will be a time of deliverance and release
from spiritual bondage *(Galatians 44:22-31; Jeremiah 33:7,11; Galatians 5:1; Psalm 126).* The
Church has been in bondage to traditions of men. A
great release in the Spirit is coming to the Church
today as it applies the New Testament principles of
discipline and life.

k)   Restoration is a time in which we can expect the
     Gospel to be preached into all the world *(Mat-
     thew 24:14).*

l)   During restoration we can expect that there will be
     a lukewarmness on the part of many to this end
     time message *(Revelation 3:15-17).*

m)   This lukewarmness will precipitate a great falling
     away in times of great pressure *(II Thessalonians 2:
     3).* This certainly does not mean that only a faith-
     ful few will remain to meet the Lord, but it does
     mean that the time is coming when those that are
     "riding the fence" in their spiritual commitment will
     be forced to make a decision one way or another.
     Many will go the way of the world, but many will
     come into a deeper life of complete consecration.

n)   Restoration will be characterized by the continual
     recovery of lost truth *(Acts 3:20-21).* The Church
     will once again experience portions of the inher-
     itance that were lost to them through unbelief,
     until the entire inheritance be possessed.

o)   As true ministries arise in this time we can also ex-
     pect false ministries to arise. These false minis-
     tries will be empowered by Satan to do many
     mighty things *(II Peter 2:1-3; Matthew 24:11. 24),*
     and will be the ambassadors of strong delusion that
     will come in the last days. Whatever God is doing,
     Satan will attempt to counterfeit. For this reason
     the people of God need to have spiritual discern-
     ment that they might try the spirits.

p)   In the last times there will be signs in the heavens
     and earth *(Matthew 24:29-30).* The earth is waxing
     old like a garment. The natural signs of this old

age will be manifested during the culmination of
history.

20. WHO WILL BE RESTORED? THE JEW? THE DEVIL?

Many Christians today believe that the Jewish people
will be restored as in the days of old. They are looking
forward to the rebuilding of the physical, material temple
as if this were some great event on God's timetable. Many
are finding great excitement in running here and there in
an effort to find clues as to the plans of the Jewish
people. What God is doing today goes much deeper than
that. When God inaugurated the Church upon the exaltation of His Son, the people of God themselves became
the temple of God. God now has a spiritual temple in
the heart of every believer. God will never leave this
temple for that natural, material temple that only pointed the way to Him who was to come.

When Christ came, He came to the Jew first. *"He came
unto His own, and His own received Him not" (John 1:11).*
Certainly there were some Jews who did accept Him *(Acts
6:7),* but for the most part the Jewish nation rejected the
message, and in turn God rejected them in 70 A.D. Up until
the coming of Christ, Israel had been likened to an Olive Tree.
This Olive Tree represented the tree of faith. When Christ
came, all those Jews that received Him by faith remained in
the tree, but all those who rejected the Son of God were cast
off. The Gospel then went forth to the Gentiles. All of those
who accepted Christ by faith were grafted into this tree of
faith, but all those who rejected Christ remained outside of
the tree. So we no longer have an ethnic tree. We have one
tree consisting of both Jew and Gentile who have one thing in
common – faith in the Lord Jesus Christ, *(Read Romans 11).*
In these times of restoration we must begin to pray that the
Jew accepts Christ, not that he is able to rebuild the temple.

*Romans 10:1 - "Brethren, my heart's desire and prayer to
God for Israel is, that they might be saved."*

*Romans 11:20-23 - "Well; because of unbelief they were
broken off, and thou standest by faith. Be not high-mind-
ed, but fear: For if God spared not the natural branches,
take heed lest he also spare not thee. Behold therefore
the goodness and severity of God: on them which fell,
severity; but toward thee, goodness, if thou continue
in his goodness: otherwise thou also shalt be cut off.
And they also, if they abide not still in unbelief, shall
be grafted in: for God is able to graft them in again."*

There are many today who are preaching other things in
regard to Restoration of which we must give a WORD OF
WARNING. Some feel that the Devil will be restored. This is
a typical example of what can result when the natural mind
begins to interpret a verse here and a verse there out of the
context of Scripture. Restoration, as we have said, will involve
only those things that were spoken by the mouth of the holy
prophets. Nowhere can you find in the Scriptures a prophetic
voice predicting the restoration of Satan. We have to be very
cautious that we do not carry these concepts any further
than God's Word takes them *(Revelation 20:10, 14)*.

21. WHAT AREAS IN PARTICULAR CAN WE EXPECT TO BE RESTORED?

Ezekiel 34 tells us the condition of God's people and
their need for restoration. The Scripture refers to at least
seven areas in which we can expect God to move in restoration.

a)   TRUTH - If God is going to fully restore His Church,
      then there is going to have to be an exposure to
      truth in a way that we have never experienced.
      Truth is the means God uses to change us. As we
      look upon the truth we are changed from glory
      to glory *(II Corinthians 3:18)*. All throughout
      Scripture truth is related to the concept of light.

God's Word is the Word of truth *(Psalm 119:43; II Corinthians 6:7; Ephesians 1:13; Colossians 1:5; II Timothy 2:15; James 1:18),* and yet it is a lamp unto our feet and a light unto our path *(Psalm 119:105).* It is exposure to this Word that brings us into the place of light *(Psalm 119:130).*

God is wanting to do a tremendous work in His Church today *(Ephesians 3:10-11; 4:11-16; Acts 3:21; Revelation 7:1-4),* but it is important for us to see that when God works, He always works in the atmosphere of light — Truth *(Genesis 1:3).* It is the ministry of the Holy Spirit, the Spirit of truth *(John 14:17); 15:26; 16:13; I John 4:6),* to create the atmosphere for the reception of truth. In the first restoration we find a condition of darkness interrupted by the Spirit brooding or hovering over the face of the deep, *"and God said, Let there be light" (Genesis 1:2-3).* In the same way the Holy Spirit can be seen in relation to the candlestick in the tabernacle of Moses. He is the oil from which that light is brought forth. The Holy Spirit has this ministry in the life of the believer also. He is the one who prepares the ground upon which that seed of truth, the seed of the Word *(Compare: Luke 8:11 and John 17:17)* may fall *(I Corinthians 12:3).*

If the end time Church is going to experience something that no other generation of believers has experienced, it must experience the light of God to open its eyes. We must experience more light than any other generation. The Holy Spirit, the Revealer of Truth, is our teacher who will lead us line upon line, precept upon precept *(Isaiah 28:10)* until we are changed into the image *(Ephesians 4:13).* This is God's method of teaching. It is always progressive.

There needs to be a restoration of truth to the Church. One doesn't have to read the New Testament too many times to know that we have lost something of the revelation and power of the Early Church. We stand with the Hebrew Christians in their need to be grounded firmly in the first principles of the doctrine of Christ *(Hebrews 6:1-3).* But beyond that we need to have an ear to hear that particular thing which God wants to do in regard to the Church of the last days. There are many truths that throughout all history have never been made manifest because they are reserved for this Church of the end time. We need to have an ear to hear what the Spirit is saying in this day.

I Peter 1:5 - "Who are kept by the power of God through faith unto salvation ready to be revealed in the last time."

Jesus said in *John 14:6, "I am the Way, the Truth, and the Life: no man cometh unto the Father, but by Me."* Jesus is the Way, the only way to salvation and eternal life. He is actually the way to a threefold salvation of spirit, soul and body *(I Thessalonians 5:23)*. When we come to know the Lord and our Spirit is born anew, we find Jesus as THE WAY. Jesus fulfills this role as the Lamb slain from the foundation of the world. *(Revelation 13:8)*.

But Jesus is also the Truth. He is renewing our souls daily after the image of the Creator *(Colossians 3:10; Romans 12:2)*. This work of redemption has to do with the mind, the will and the emotions, or, we could say, the soul of man *(Ephesians 4:23; II Corinthians 4:16)*. As we submit to this renewing process we experience Jesus as THE TRUTH. Jesus fulfills this role as our baptizer with the Holy Ghost and fire *(Matthew 3:11, 12)*.

Jesus also told us that He is the Life. This has to do with the aspect of salvation that is waiting to be revealed in the last days *(I Peter 1:5)*. This has to do with an experience of the life of God *(I Corinthians 15:51-58)*. This has to do with the revelation of the life of Christ flowing to the Church and supplying that resurrection life and translation power to the people of God. When this becomes a part of the Christian experience we will experience Jesus as THE LIFE. Jesus fulfills this role in His ministry as our Great High Priest *(Hebrews 7:15-16)*.

III John 4 - "I have no greater joy than to hear that my children walk in the truth."

b) MINISTRIES - After God restores a truth He will
always   have prepared, true ministries to administrate that truth. If a truth does not come under
proper guidance and ministry, it can be dangerous.
All one has to do is see how some of the modern
day movements have perverted a genuine Bible truth
to the exclusion of the natural checks and balances
in the rest of the Scripture to see the importance of
God-directed ministries. There is a tremendous
need for skilled workmen to rightly divide the Word
of Truth. God is restoring the five-fold ministry of
apostles, prophets, evangelists, pastors and teachers
for the perfecting of the saints, until we all come to
the unity of the faith *(Ephesians 4:11-16)*. The
Church cannot be perfected without the five gifted
or ascension gift ministries. They are God's gift to
the Church.

As God works in restoration therefore, we can expect
that God will be preparing the proper leadership beforehand,
so that there will be skilled workmen to lead the people in.
There will be a restoration of the husbandmen *(Jeremiah
31:14, 24-26)* who have received from the Lord and are,
consequently, able to cause the flock to lie down *(Jeremiah
33:12-13)*. From this type of ministry there will be growth,
because the flock will be fed and satisfied. Jesus is the Great
Shepherd *(John 10:1)* who sets the pattern for all true shepherds of the sheepfold, the Church.

God is at the present time raising up these ministries and
Isaiah 30:20-21 is being fulfilled:

*Isaiah 30:20-21 - "And though the Lord give you the
bread of adversity, and the water of affliction, yet shall
not thy teachers be removed into a corner any more,
but thine eyes shall see thy teachers: And thine ears
shall hear a word behind thee, saying, This is the way,
walk ye in it, when ye turn to the right hand and when
ye turn to the left."*

c)   PEOPLE - During the Dark Ages and in any captivity, natural or spiritual, God's people are in a condition of being robbed and spoiled. Their bones are
picked clean by the birds of the air, and there is
the smell of death and defeat. But God promises
that as His people look to Him He will build them
up *(Jeremiah 31:4)*. There was a plucking up, a
pulling down and a destruction that came to the
Church in the Dark Ages, but God promises that the
nation that repents and turns from their evil He will
again build and plant in a watered place *(Isaiah 58:
11)*.

The Church was like those dry bones in *Ezekiel (37:1)*
that had been picked clean by the theological buzzards of the
day. They had the theological framework, but there was
no life on the bones. As God visits His people, these bones
have the potential of becoming the restored Body of Christ.
God promises to make the bones of His people fat once again
(Isaiah 58:11), they shall be like a watered garden, and they
shall *"flourish like an herb" (Isaiah 66:14)*. The people of God
are now being restored. God is restoring our soul and leading
us beside still waters. He is preparing a table before us wherein is life and health, both naturally and spiritually *(Psalm 23)*.

d)   WORSHIP - True worship in Spirit and Truth can
only come from the lips of a people who have
experienced the two witnesses of the Spirit and the
Truth *(John 4:23-24)*. This is the natural expression on the lips of a people who have been restored
and who are walking in the light of His Presence
wherein is fulness of joy *(Jeremiah 31:12)*. The
voice of the end-time Church will be saying, *"Praise
the Lord of Hosts" (Jeremiah 33:11)*, because it
consists of a people who know the importance of
bringing their spiritual sacrifices of praise into the
House of the Lord *(Hebrews 13:15)*.

The Church of God is to be His habitation by the Spirit *(Ephesians 2:21-22)*, and we know that God inhabits the praises of His people *(Psalm 22:3)*. It is clear that a restoration of true worship to the Church implies a restoration of the Presence of the Lord to His House. God is building up Zion, the Church of the Firstborn *(Hebrews 12:22-23)*. Zion is where the Tabernacle of David was established which was the place of audible praise. It is this generation that shall praise the Lord; it is this generation that shall break the appointment with death *(Psalm 102:16-20)*.

Jeremiah 31:12-13 - "Therefore shall they come and sing in the height of Zion, and shall flow together to the goodness of the Lord, for wheat, and for wine, and for oil, and for the young of the flock and of the herd: and their soul shall be as a watered garden; and they shall not sorrow any more at all. Then shall the virgin rejoice in the dance, both young men and old together for I will turn their mourning into joy, and will comfort them, and make them rejoice from their sorrow."

e) PATHS TO DWELL IN - God promises to restore the paths in which to dwell. This message of restoration leads to a deeper life in our daily experience. God is restoring practical principles to the individual, to the family and to the Church; for the cry is going out, "get your house in order!" As we begin to apply God's principles to our every day life, we will see a restoration of personal relationships and life experiences that we never dreamed possible.

Isaiah 58:12 - "And they that shall be of thee shall build the old waste places: thou shalt raise up the foundations of many generations; and thou shalt be called, the repairer of the breach, the restorer of paths to dwell in."

The decline of the Church began as a gap began to form between doctrine and experience. Many of the doctrines of the Church remained scriptural, but there was no corresponding experience in the life of the average believer. It was as if they were burning incense to vanity (worshipping useless things), because they stumbled from the PATH of truth *(Jeremiah 18:15)*. As time went on in this subnormal level, even some of the great landmarks of doctrine were erased to measure up with the experience of the average person *(Job 24:2-4)*. In so doing they rebelled against the light and were brought further out of the path *(Job 24:13)*.

God has promised to restore these pathways and re-establish the land-marks *(Jeremiah 31:21)*. He is doing this in His Church, the place of safety, the Sheepfold. The Church should be the center of all activity of the Church flock, spiritually and naturally. All recreation, fun and fellowship for young and old should come from the Church under the canopy of God's Glory and the Shepherd's Rod. God is revealing this as the way, and He is instructing us *"to walk in it" (Isaiah 30:21)*.

f)   YEARS - As the Church went into decline, we see that many years of history have been eaten up by backsliding and lack of progress. There are many individual Christians who have had similar experiences on a personal level. There are ministers of the Gospel who know that for many years they were functioning in partial light. But God has promised to restore the years that were lost *(Joel 2: 25)*. He promises that the glory of the later House will be greater than the glory of the former House *(Haggai 2:9)*. He promises that the end of a thing is better than the beginning *(Ecclesiastes 7:8)*. He gives us the picture of Samson, who did more in his last exploit than he did in all his other exploits put together *(Judges 16:30)*.

g)   KINGDOM - We can expect that these days of restoration will prepare the way for the Kingdom to come *(Matthew 6:10)*. It will come as the laws of the Kingdom begin to be put into operation by the people of God. Jesus taught His disciples principles for Kingdom living *(Matthew 5-7)*. As the Church learns to live in those things involved in the restoration of truth, ministries, people, paths, worship and years, we will see a full restoration of God's Kingdom on earth. The fulness of all these are yet to come, but we can be instrumental in bringing that Kingdom by praying for it and doing what we can to get our lives in order. *"For the Kingdom of God is not meat and drink; but righteousness, and peace, and joy in the Holy Ghost"(Romans 14:17)*.

This Kingdom will be victorious over all other spiritual or earthly kingdoms and will ultimately be delivered to the Father *(I Corinthians 15:24)*. It is an eternal Kingdom that God is restoring.

STUDY QUESTIONS FOR CHAPTER THREE

1.   Define the term "restoration".

2.   What three things are involved in restoration?

3.   List four Old Testament passages that deal with restoration.

4.   What three things does *Acts 3:21* tell us about restoration?

5.   List ten things that will characterize times of restoration.

6.   Is there a limit as to what will be restored? What is it?

7.   List six things that we can expect to be restored?

CHAPTER FOUR

*The Church From Its Decline
To Its Power*

The Church
From Its Decline
To Its Power
Chapter Four

As we have seen, the Church that began exhibiting great spiritual power declined to a place of dead formalism. The Church had been robbed of its spiritual heritage in Christ and "none said, Restore." The clergy of the Middle Ages was for the most part corrupt, and they knew not the ways of the Lord. It was similar to the condition to which the Aaronic priesthood had fallen during the period of the Judges. A generation arose that did not know the Lord, and it was led by a priesthood that did not fear the Lord or have respect to His ways.

As the book of *I Samuel* begins, we find that the high priest of Israel is a man by the name of Eli. Eli is old, overweight, nearly blind and has two immoral sons. His sons were so perverse that they would lay with the women who came to offer sacrifices at the door of the Tabernacle *(I Samuel 2:22)*. This is the condition of the nation as a whole. The high priest, who is to be the spiritual leader of the nation, doesn't even have his own sons under control.

We are told that the Word of the Lord was precious or scarce in those days *(I Samuel 3:1)*. Because of this situation, the people, in general, had no vision or understanding of what God wanted to do *(I Samuel 3:1)*. Things looked very dim for the people of God. The future looked dark because the light of God's truth was going out. But, thanks be to God, there was a faithful remnant of praying people who still believed God. There were women like Hannah who still looked to God to move among His people. It was people like Hannah who were constant in prayer that preserved the flame of truth. Before the lamp of God's truth was completely extinguished, the Lord called to a young man by the name of Samuel *(I Samuel 3:3-4)*. This was the start of a revival and a restoration of the things of God, for we know that Samuel was one of the purest ministries in the Old Testament.

This is precisely what happened in regard to the Church. The Dark Ages left the Church in a condition in which the official priesthood did not fear the Lord or inquire into His ways. The Church had lost the Spirit, and the great truths of God's Word were no longer experienced in the life of the average Church-goer. But God is faithful. He never lets the light of His truth go completely out. In every generation there has been a faithful remnant of believers who were not afraid to ask God for visitation. As prayer ascended, before the lamp of truth went completely out, God called to a man named Martin Luther, and the valley of dry bones began to move *(Ezekiel 37)*.

In this chapter we would like to see how God began to move to fulfill His promise to restore the Church.

22. HOW HAS GOD BEEN FULFILLING HIS PROMISES OF RESTORATION IN THE CHURCH?

God has been restoring truth to the Church in nearly the same order as the Church lost the truth. The prophet Joel gives us a good prophetic picture of what God is to do in the last days. As he begins his prophecy, he summarizes what has taken place in relation to the loss of truth.

Joel 1:4 - "That which the palmerworm hath left hath the locust eaten; and that which the locust hath left hath the cankerworm eaten; and that which the cankerworm hath left hath the caterpillar eaten."

Joel pictures the decline of truth as the stripping away of foliage by the different stages of an insect. He tells us that the palmerworm has eaten. The palmerworm is the larvae stage of the insect, and is only a little worm that eats very little. From a distance one may not even be able to see the effect of its eating at all, but it is the beginning of something devastating. It is not a matter of how much this worm eats, but it is the potential threat of this worms later stages. If this little worm goes unchecked it will cause deep problems, for the palmerwom gives way to the caterpillar which lives on the small tender leaves. The caterpillar gives way to the canker-worm, a larger worm that eats the leaves and bores into the bark. Finally, the fully developed locust emerges which eats everything, the bark, the trees, the vines, and all vegetation. It will leave a trail of death. The tragedy of it is that if this process is unchecked, locusts have the potential of producing more locusts. The locusts that eat away at the life of the Church include bitterness, criticism, discontent, laziness and unfaithfulness. In the embryo stage they may seem harmless, but they have all the potential of destroying life.

This is the condition of the Church as we find it in 1500. As the tree of God, it has been stripped of all life. But Joel becomes the mouthpiece of God's promise to the Church to restore all that these insects have eaten.

> *Joel 2:23-26 - "Be glad then, ye children of Zion, and rejoice in the Lord your God: for He hath given you the former rain moderately, and He will cause to come for you the rain, the former rain, and the latter rain in the first month. And the floors shall be full of wheat, and the vats shall overflow with wine and oil. And I will restore to you the years that the locust hath eaten, the cankerworm, and the caterpillar, and the palmer-worm, my great army which I sent among you. And ye shall eat in plenty, and be satisfied, and praise the name of the Lord your God, and none else: and My people shall never be ashamed."*

(Note: Carefully examine the chart on the following page in connection with Joel's prophecy, and continually refer to it as we discuss the restoration of the Church).

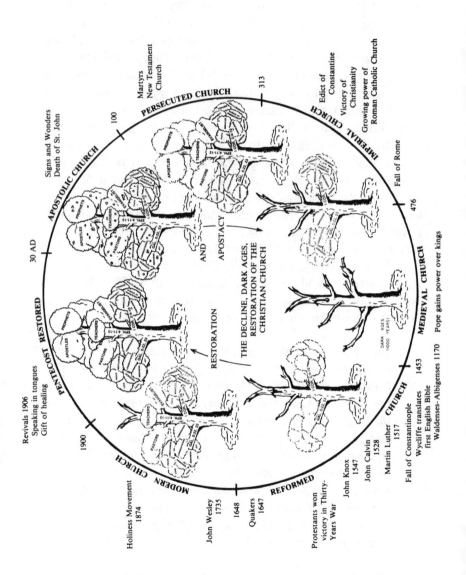

23. HOW DID GOD BEGIN TO RESTORE THE CHURCH?

God began to restore the Church by restoring the most foundational truth in the Christian experience first. God restored the truth of justification by faith in Jesus Christ. Until a man comes and drinks from the well of salvation, all other pursuits are meaningless. The unregenerate cannot understand the things of God, neither can he know them. And so it was in the early 16th Century that God singled out a vessel to use for His glory. This vessel was Martin Luther.

Martin Luther was a very well educated young man who had begun his education in the area of law. During his study he was troubled in his spirit by certain eternal questions that as yet had not been answered for him. He was a Church member, but he lacked any assurance of his personal salvation. This deep spiritual concern drove him to abandon his law career and join a monastery where he hoped to find the answers to his many questions.

As Martin Luther continued his study he was struck by his utter unworthiness and sinful condition. In order to appease or placate a righteous God and his troubled conscience he fasted, beat himself and did every good work that was suggested to him. Nothing he did brought peace to his soul. Frustrated beyond measure Luther declared that he could not love a God who demanded such from men.

As Luther continued to contend for inner peace, he was encouraged to make a pilgrimage to Rome, the Holy City, where "his faith would be inspired". Rome was the center of religiosity. It offered many means of indulgence to the sinner. It was as Luther visited Rome and watched and listened and joined with the people in doing righteous acts that he began to question the value of such works. One day as he climbed the steps of St. Peter's Cathedral, repeating the Lord's Prayer on every step in order to deliver his grandfather from purgatory, the question came to him, "Who knows whether this is true?"

At this point he began to look critically at many of the traditions of the Church. He was especially shocked at the use of indulgences to free men from the responsibility of leading godly lives. In 1517, as he began to cry out to God, God met him. As he was reading *Romans 1:16-17,* God by His Spirit reached down and quickened the Word of Truth, and Luther realized for the first time that *"the just shall live by faith".*

Luther honestly believed that this was all so simple and clear that as soon as he shared what he had discovered, the Church would see it immediately, and everyone would experience personal salvation as he had. It was not so. Many people did receive what Luther taught, but the official Roman Church condemned him.

Luther preached against many of the doctrines that had caused the decline of the Church. He taught that Christ alone was the Mediator between God and man. He taught that indulgences meant nothing to God, and that repentant Christians could receive full forgiveness as they came to Christ in faith. He denied that the pope and the clergy had any supernatural priestly power, and reaffirmed the doctrine of the priesthood of all believers. He denied that only the pope could interpret the Scripture and stated that any true believer could search the Scripture *(II Timothy 2:15; II Peter 1:20).* He went so far as to say that any believer armed with the Scripture was mightier and had more authority than any pope without it.

As oppostion arose all around Luther and his associates, there was much work done in the area of doctrinal definition. Most of this work was done to present a scriptural defence of their position. As time went on, however, these formulations became creeds and a new Church was born. Luther never intended or desired to separate the Church, but, as the poles spread further and further apart, a separation was affected. This became known as the Lutheran Church.

24. WHAT FOLLOWED THE MESSAGE OF JUSTIFICATION BY FAITH?

Just seven short years after God opened the eyes of Martin Luther to the truth of justification by faith, God began to reveal the next line of truth to some followers of Luther. As men like Hubmaier, Grebel and Manz began to look to the Lord, they began to doubt the validity of infant baptism. If salvation truly came by faith, how could infants who have no profession of faith be administered baptism? It was not long before these men translated their theory into practice and re-instituted believer's baptism by immersion. More and more believers saw the truth of water baptism and followed them into the water. Soon these believers, who were outcasts to the religious society of the day, began to form their own Churches and withdraw from others in society.

This group became known as the Anabaptists or "rebaptized". A more appropriate title would be "Baptists", since they felt they had been properly baptized only once. This group received tremendous persecution from both the Lutherans and the Catholics for this practice. Lutherans, who themselves were being persecuted by Catholics, joined forces against the Anabaptists and, in the pretense of giving them the rite of water baptism, held them under the water until they drowned.

What a tragedy! The same group that had just heard the voice of God and had responded positively now closed their ears to the next thing that God was saying. The leaders of the visitation of 1517 became the persecutors of the subsequent visitation. God was visiting His people with more truth, but many were not open to it.

In regard to the doctrine of baptism there were four main issues that were involved.

a)   Baptism itself was now believed to be properly administered only by immersion. This is the only method known to the New Testament *(Matthew 3: 16; Acts 8:38; John 3:23).*

b)   Baptism was to be experienced only by those who had repented and acknowledged faith in the Lord Jesus Christ *(Acts 2:38; 8:37)*. An infant cannot repent; neither can he believe with all his heart.

c)   Baptism was regarded as an act of obedience to the Word of Christ *(Matthew 28:19; Romans 6:16-17; 5:19)*. If you really have faith in God you will do what He says.

d)   Baptism involves the first step in sanctification. The water is a cleansing agent in the life of the believer *(Acts 22:16)* from which we receive the power to rise to newness of life *(Romans 6:3-5)*.

25. WHAT DO WE KNOW ABOUT GOD'S NEXT MOVE TO RESTORE TRUTH?

For a period of about two hundred years there seems to have been a quiet period. God had moved to restore some tremendously important truth. But there is more to the Christian experience than salvation and water baptism. Perhaps it took two hundred years for men to realize this. Although each revival or visitation was characterized by an emphasis on living a holy life, we notice that the farther we get from the event, the more reckless lives become. This is what happened in this period of two hundred years. Although many moved into the experience of salvation and water baptism, they found certain problems in living an overcoming life above circumstances.

As more and more people saw this discrepency between the profession of faith and the life of the average Christian, they began to seek God for answers. They began to seek God for a deeper experience. They began hungering and thirsting after righteousness. Every visitation is watered by prayer. As men set themselves to seek the Lord, God began to speak.

All over the world God was beginning to lay stress on another area of the Christian experience. God singled out men like Philipp Spener in the late 17th Century. Men who began to preach that there was more to the Christian life than doctrinal correctness. There was more to the Christian experience then regular Church attendance. There was a need to separate oneself from the world. This move in Germany was called the Pietistic movement which was to lay the foundation for a renewed and restored emphasis on holiness.

Holiness was the message of the hour. God was blowing another trumpet of truth, revealing another area into which the Church needed to enter. He used many instruments to proclaim the word, Franke, Spener, Zinzendorf and Whitefield; but by far the greatest was a man named John Wesley.

John Wesley, who was strongly influenced by the Moravian Christians, experienced salvation by faith in 1738 while reading some of Luther's writings on Romans. As he studied God's Word he realized that there was more to the Christian life than what he had. He saw a tremendous lack of Bible Christians living a life style different from that of the world. He saw very little contrast between the kingdom of darkness and the Kingdom of Light.

The more John Wesley studied God's Word, the more he realized that Christ had not only provided a place for us in eternity, but that He offered a new and glorious life in the present. He believed that without holiness no man shall see the Lord *(Hebrews 12:14)*. He came to the conviction that as a Christian looked to the Lord and sought after righteousness, he could attain right ruling motives. He could attain love to God and his neighbor. Such attainment, Wesley believed would free one from sin.

John Wesley began to preach with a new zeal and a renewed emphasis. People had become complacent in their Christianity, accepting a life of defeat. John Wesley preached that we are responsible for how we live. If we are in Christ we are new creatures, and we have the responsibility to live as new creatures. Wesley preached like, perhaps, no man has ever preached. He preached three times a day to crowds running up to 20,000. The power of God was so mighty upon him that thousands would fall to the ground as conviction of sin swept over the crowds. There was a call to repentance, a call to lead a holy and a separate life.

Many Christians responded to the message of holiness, but many rejected what God was saying in those days. They missed their day of visitation and became persecutors of the truth. A tragic thing had happened in those two hundred quiet years. Churches had so locked themselves in by their exclusive doctrinal statements, that when God shed more light on truth that had been lost to the Church, there was no room in the constitution for it. Rather than change or expand their carefully worded creeds for which they had fought and died, they chose to reject the present truth.

But God was still moving, and all who moved with God saw increase. Many Christians found a new life of victory by walking through this restored door of truth. They began to understand principles of prayer and fasting. They learned to seek God for direction. They learned how to set themselves apart for the Gospel. They learned how to discipline themselves for Christ. Because of this discipline and this characteristic of being methodical in Bible study, prayer and Christian living, they became known as the Methodists.

(Note: For Scripture verses relating to the subject of holiness, see the following: *Hebrews 2:11; 12:10; Romans 12:1-2; I Peter 1:5-6; 3:15; John 17:17-19; Philippians 3: 7-10; Acts 20:32.)*

26. WHAT TRUTH DID GOD RESTORE AFTER WESLEY?

Even though men may get complacent and settled down in a truth, God never does. God has a plan, and He continues to move toward His goal in His dealings with man. About one hundred years after Wesley had called the people to repentance and separation, God moved again to restore more of the Church's lost inheritance. By His Spirit He stirred the hearts of men like A.J. Gordon,

F.B. Meyer, Andrew Murray and R.A. Torrey. He also stirred up a Presbyterian minister by the name of Albert Benjamin Simpson (1844 - 1919).

Simpson had been called to be a minister in 1865 and had ministered for about ten years. At the end of this time he experienced a profound renewal of relationship with his living Saviour. He came into what he termed the "fulness of the blessing of Christ", or sanctification "through faith in the provision of the atonement". Whatever his experience, it revolutionized his Christian life.

With his tremendous zeal for the Lord, he soon overworked himself, and his health gave out completely. It was during this time that he searched the Scriptures in regard to the nature of man, the nature of sin, and our position as believers in Christ. He saw man as consisting of a two-fold nature. He saw him as being both a material and a spiritual being. Both natures had been equally affected by the Fall, His body was exposed to disease; his soul was corrupted by sin. The more he studied, the more he believed that God had made provision for our sin-sick soul AND for the sicknesses and diseases relating to the body. God confirmed this word to him by healing him and extending his ministry another 35 years. God was restoring the truth of divine healing to the Church.

Simpson preached and wrote about what God had shown him. He had tremendous success in healing campaigns. He founded the Christian Missionary Alliance. He proclaimed what he called the "four-fold Gospel", Jesus Christ as "Saviour, Sanctifier, Healer, and Coming King". The following are some principles of divine healing that are taken from his book, "The Gospel of Healing".

a)   The causes of disease and suffering are distinctly traced to the Fall and sinful state of man. If sickness were part of the natural constitution of things then we might meet it wholly on natural grounds, and by natural means.

b)   If the disease be the result of the Fall, we may ex-
      pect it to be embraced in the provision of Redemp-
      tion.

c)   In Christ's life on earth we see a complete vision of
      what Christianity should be, and from His Words
      and works we may surely gather the full plan of
      redemption.

d)   But redemption finds its center in the Cross of our
      Lord Jesus Christ, and there we must look for the
      fundamental principles of Divine healing.

e)   But there is something ever higher than the Cross.
      It is the resurrection of our Lord. There the Gospel
      of healing finds the foundation of its deepest life.
      The death of Christ destroys sin—the root of sick-
      ness, but it is the life of Jesus which supplies the
      source of health and life for our redeemed bodies.

f)   In Christ there must be a wholly new life. If any
      man be in Christ, he is a new creature.

g)   Physical redemption that Christ brings is not merely
      healing, but also life.

h)   The great agent in bringing this new life into our life
      is the Holy Spirit. This is why many find it hard to
      meet the Healer. They do not know the Holy Spirit.

i)   This new life must come, like all the blessings of
      Christ's redemption, as the free grace of God, with-
      out works, and without distinction of merit or
      respect of persons.

j)   The simple condition of this great blessing is faith
      without sight. As with Abraham, an act of faith is
      required to appropriate the gift.

k)   Is not the Gospel of salvation a commandment as well as a promise? And is not the Gospel of healing of equal authority?

The principles of healing can be found throughout the Scripture. We know the Early Church functioned in this area, but it took the Spirit to quicken this truth afresh to the Church in the late 19th Century. There are many who rejected what God gave to A.B. Simpson. But Simpson was safe, because what God had given him was not his own idea, but it was a concept or a truth that was thoroughly based on the Word of God. A scriptural framework for the truth of healing might include the following:

a)   *Exodus 15:25-26* - This is the first promise of healing. We notice that sickness belongs to Egypt (Compare *Psalm 105:37*).

b)   *Psalm 103:2-3* - God, not man, is the deliverer of human affliction.

c)   *Isaiah 53:4-5* - Provision was made for our sickness at Calvary (Compare: *Matthew 8:16-17 and I Peter 2:24)*.

d)   *I Corinthians 11:30* -There is something that Christ left with us to supply this need.

e)   *Ephesians 5:30* - Christ's body was sickless, and we have become partakers of His flesh and bones.

f)   *Romans 8:11* - This is not a future resurrection, but it is a present reality.

g)   *Hebrews 13:8* - This is for all generations of believers, because God does not change His Word.

h)   *James 5:14* - We have a commission to heal given at the close of the Apostolic Age. It is more than a privilege, it is a command!

27. WHAT HAPPENED A FEW SHORT YEARS AFTER SIMPSON'S DISCOVERY?

Around the same time God was moving in mighty ways all through the earth. Sincere Christians everywhere were praying, fasting and seeking God for further visitation. In 1904-05 the Welsh revival broke out. This seems to have been a real spark for something that had already been smoldering in America. For several years there had been an urgency among many of God's people that God was about to move. God confirmed these feelings by a sporatic outpouring of the Spirit. In 1896 in a small group in North Carolina, God opened heaven's windows and poured out of His Spirit, and men began to prophesy and speak with other tongues. In 1901 God did the same thing to a group of believers in Topeka, Kansas, setting the stage for a great outpouring a few years later.

In 1906 in Los Angeles during the now famous Azusa Street revivals, God poured out of His Spirit in a miraculous way. As Frederick Bruner puts it, "At the Azusa Street meetings the Pentecostal movement ignited. Its fires were apparently so intense that they were felt within a short time around the world. The conflagration swept first across America itself."

It was a tremendous day of Pentecost for the Church. All former revivals had been stirring mainly in the intellect and the inner man with no outward manifestation. God has been laying a foundation of true, deep reverence towards God upon which He could build true joy manifested in outward demonstration. There is no true joy without a deep reverence for God. Any physical manifestation apart from this deep reverence for God is simply a display of flesh.

As God poured out of His Spirit and men spoke in other tongues and prophesied, there was great commotion in religious circles. There was a violent reaction against such outward display of emotion. Perhaps more than any other visitation, these Christians who had received the Baptism with the Holy Spirit with the evidence of speaking in tongues were persecuted by other Christians who had not received the experience. These "tongue-talkers" were ex-communicated from their various churches and were bitterly opposed.

The central doctrine of this move was the Baptism of the Holy Spirit with the evidence of speaking in tongues. A scriptural framework of this truth might include the following:

a) *Joel 2:28* - The Old Testament prophets foretold of the coming of this experience *(Acts 2:16-18, also Isaiah 28:11-12).*

b) *Matthew 3:11-12* - It was proclaimed by John to be part of the ministry of Jesus to administer this baptism *(Mark 1:7-8; Luke 3:16).* Some confuse this Holy Spirit baptism with water baptism. It is interesting that Jesus never water baptized anyone *(John 4:1-2).* He had a different baptism to administer.

c) *Matthew 3:16* - Jesus Himself experienced this endowment after His baptism in the Jordan *(Mark 1:9-11; Luke 3:21-22).*

d) *John 7:37-39* - Jesus Himself foretold this experience *(Mark 16:17).*

e) *Acts 2:1-13* - The disciples experienced the baptism of the Holy Ghost on the Day of Pentecost (See: *Acts 1:8; Luke 24:49).*

f) *Acts 2:38* - The message of this baptim was preached by the apostles *(Acts 2:38),* and it is, therefore, part of the apostles doctrine *(Acts 2:42).*

g) *Acts 9:17-18* - Paul experienced the Baptism of the Holy Spirit (Connect: *I Corinthians 14:18)*.

h) It was experienced by the Samaritans, the House of Cornelius and the Ephesians *(Acts 8:14-18; 10:44-48; 19:1-6)*.

i) It is to be experienced TODAY *(Acts 2:38-39; Mark 16:17; Hebrews 13:8)!* It is a dangerous thing when we start dispensationalizing portions of Scripture.

j) It is the downpayment of an even fuller experience yet to come *(Ephesians 1:13-14)*.

k) It is accompanied by tongues (Examine scriptures in connection with letters e, g, and h). God wants to get control of our tongue, so that He might get control of the entire vessel *(James 3:1-10)*. At the same time He wants us to receive edification that we could not get in any other way *(I Corinthians 14:4, 14-15; Ephesians 6:18; Jude 20)*. Tongues are also given for spiritual intercession *(Romans 8:26)*.

l) *Luke 11:10-13* - God is no respecter of persons. It is His desire that all of His children receive this gift. As with any gift, it is not earned, it is given *(Romans 6:13)*.

m) *Ephesians 5:18* - It is a command of the Lord!

With this quickening of the truth of the Baptism of the Holy Spirit, there also came a renewed emphhasis on the gifts and fruit of the Spirit. The gifts of the Spirit are given by the grace of God, and the fruit is worked into the character of the Christian by a gradual process. Both of these are made more evident in the life of the believer who has experienced the Baptism of the Spirit.

The Gifts of the Spirit are discussed in depth in *I Corinthians 12*. Here Paul tells us that there are different kinds of gifts, but the same Spirit is involved in all of them *(12:4)*. He says that there are different operations, but the same Lord *(12:4)*. He further says that a manifestation of the Spirit is given to EVERY man for the profit of the whole body *(12:7)*. He continues by listing the nine gifts, exhorting us in the operation of these gifts and in conclusion exhorts us to desire spiritual gifts *(12:31)*. The nine gifts listed by Paul could be easily divided into three groups of three, as follows:

a)   SPIRITUAL REVELATION

   1)   THE WORD OF WISDOM - this gift is an unearned and supernatural impartation of a fragment of God's total wisdom to meet a particular need, answer a particular challenge or utilize a particular piece of knowledge.

   2)   THE WORD OF KNOWLEDGE - The gift of the word of knowledge is the God-given ability to receive from God, by revelation, facts and information which is humanly impossible to know.

   3)   DISCERNING OF SPIRITS - The gift of discerning of spirits is the God-given ability to recognize what spirit is behind different manifestations or activities *(Acts 16:18)*.

b)   GIFTS OF POWER

   1)   FAITH - The gift of faith is the God-given ability to believe God for the impossible *(Acts 6:8 not Romans 12:3)*.

   2)   WORKING OF MIRACLES - The gift of miracles is the God-given ability to perform the impossible.

3)   GIFTS OF HEALING - The gifts of healing are given by God to impart healing for the physical body at certain specific times.

c)   GIFTS OF UTTERANCE

1)   DIVERS KINDS OF TONGUES - The gift of tongues is a God-given ability which enables a believer to speak in a language which he doesn't know *(I Corinthians 14:22)*.

2)   INTERPRETATION OF TONGUES - The gift of the interpretation of tongues is the God-given ability to bring forth in a known tongue a message that was given in an unknown tongue.

3)   PROPHECY - Prophecy is the God-given ability to speak forth a message from God in a known tongue which you have received directly from the Holy Spirit for the particular situation. This will involve both forthtelling and foretelling.

All of these gifts are supernatural and unearned. Although an individual may have an extensive ministry in one of the gifts, they are given by God to the body of Christ to meet a particular need. The fruit of the Spirit is quite different. The fruit involves those graces of character that are worked into the life of every believer who yields his members to the influence and work of the Holy Spirit. This fruit of the Spirit described in *Galatians* is also nine-fold.

a)   LOVE - We are to love others with a God-like love *(I Corinthians 13)*.

b)   JOY - Love brings forth joy *(John 15:10 - 11)*.

c)   PEACE - Peace involves a rest and relaxation and a freedom from tormenting thoughts, worries and fears.

d)   LONGSUFFERING - Longsuffering could be equated with patient endurance, waiting for God to fulfill His Word in His time.

e) GENTLENESS - The Spirit works gentleness into our lives so that we are not harsh or pushy to get our own way.

f) GOODNESS - The Spirit controlled life manifests that which is helping and edifying to others.

g) FAITH - The Spirit helps us to move or grow from faith to faith.

h) MEEKNESS - Since we have given over our rights to the Lord, we have nothing to defend. We are freed to live a mild, humble, disciplined and flexible life.

i) TEMPERANCE - The Spirit is able to bring self under control so that it will not be free to indulge in that which brings evil.

(Note: For a more complete study of these areas in connection with the Baptism, the gifts and the fruit of the Holy Spirit, see "THE HOLY SPIRIT TODAY", by K.R. Iverson.)

28. WHAT IS GOD'S PURPOSE IN ALL THESE DEALINGS WITH THE CHURCH?

God is not just dealing with the Church in this manner because of a lack of something better to do. God has a glorious plan which He is in the process of working out in His dealings with man. Each new visitation brings us just that much closer to the end product. Each new step or portion of truth brings us ever closer to that fully restored Church that will be a fit or suitable Bride for His Son. The Church will indeed be a help MEET for the Son of God. It will be a glorious Church without spot or wrinkle or any such thing *(Ephesians 5:27)*.

God is going to have a Church who will measure up to the Divine standard. He will have a Bride for His Son. This is why it is so important for us to listen closely to what God has to say to us in this hour, for it will bring us closer to the ultimate goal of the Church of Jesus Christ. Sad to say, many reject the dealings of God, and miss out on the blessing. When they reject what God is saying, they miss out on God's perfect plan for them.

God is moving by His Spirit in these days. He is restoring truth. As He restores truth in which the Church has never walked, He also adds depth to the things that we have already experienced. God restored water baptism to the Church many centuries ago, and yet, He is still adding depth to that experience as He teaches us about the name of the Lord Jesus Christ and the circumcision of the heart. God is moving. The safest and most glorious place is to move with God!

29. WHY ARE THERE SO MANY DIFFERENT CHURCHES TODAY?

When we get a glimpse of what God is doing in terms of His eternal purpose and plan, it is not hard for us to see why there are so many Churches in this day. This is a question that is asked by multitudes today. To many it is a stumbling block to their acceptance of Christianity. But in light of what we have seen throughout Church history, the answer is evident.

Whenever God begins to restore lost truth to the Church there are at least two reactions by the people of God. Some people receive it, and some people reject it. This is what happened in Luther's day. God desired to restore justification by faith to the Church. Some people gladly received the Word and moved into the experience of what God was doing. But, alas, others rejected God's moving and continued in their traditions.

The followers of Luther reformed all the old creeds and formal statements on the basis of the new experience that they had come to know. They set down their doctrines in formulas which became the test for pure doctrine. But God was not finished restoring His Church. He was not finished speaking to them.

Soon God spoke again. God said, "He that believeth and is baptized shall be saved". Many of the Lutherans gladly received this truth and moved with the voice of God. Others looked and examined their creedal statements, and when they found no room for this novel doctrine, they refused to move. Of course there was no room in their creeds for this experience. It had been lost to the Church for over 1000 years!

This, then became the primary cause for the divisions among Christendom. When men make creeds, they box themselves in, and they close off any possibility of God adding to the truth He has once given. What a tragedy that nearly every Church that began by responding to the voice of God in restoration closed itself off to further revelation by formulating closed creeds. We must know what we believe and be able to formulate it. But we must not allow that creed to overrule what God may have to say to us as He moves to restore lost truth to the Church. As we move with God, we will move from glory to glory!

STUDY QUESTIONS FOR CHAPTER FOUR

1. What picture does the prophet Joel give us of restoration?

2. What was the first thing that God restored to the Church?

3. As God began to deal in the area of water baptism, what four issues came to the surface?

4. What teaching of Wesley causes him to stand out in restoration history?

5. Give a scriptural outline of the doctrine of healing.

6. Give a scriptural outline of the Baptism of the Holy Spirit.

7. List the nine gifts of the Spirit mentioned in *I Corinthians 12*.

8. What is the nine-fold fruit of the Spirit?

9. What is the basic difference between the gifts and the fruit of the Spirit?

10. What danger do we see in each of these movements that were initiated by God?

CHAPTER FIVE

God's Present Visitation

God's Present Visitation

Chapter Five

In *Genesis 1:2-3* we are given a beautiful picture of how God brought order out of chaos. The earth was without form and void, and darkness was upon the face of the deep. But God was not oblivious to the situation. Before any visible change in this darkened condition occured, the Spirit of God moved upon the face of the waters. The Spirit of God was preparing the way for the Word of God to bring deliverance, *"And God said, Let there be light: and there was light" (Genesis 1:3).*

The Church of the Middle Ages was dwelling in darkness. It was dwelling in the darkness of human traditions and human ceremonies. But God was not oblivious to the situation. He sent forth His Spirit into the world to draw wayward men back to the Word, the Lord Jesus Christ. The Spirit of God moved upon the darkness of the Dark Ages and God said, *"The just shall live by faith!"*

The days of creation are a beautiful type of the restoration of the Church. The restoration that takes place in *Genesis 1* begins with God calling the world out of darkness into marvelous light. This light then becomes foundational to all that follows, for no life can exist where there is no light. This is exactly what God did in relation to the Church. With Martin Luther, God called the church out of darkness into His marvelous light. Without the light that God provides, there can be no spiritual life. Jesus came as the life, and the life was the light of men *(John 1:4).* In the experience of the individual, the light is received when we receive Christ as our Lord and Saviour. In the restoration of the Church, the light came through the recovery of the truth of SALVATION by faith in the Lord Jesus Christ.

The days of creation proceed to unfold a picture of the further restoration of truth. On the second day there was a division of the waters, speaking of water baptism where we are divided or separated unto the Lord. The days continue until we come to the sixth day on which God created a MAN IN HIS IMAGE *(Genesis 1:26-28)*. These thoughts have been summarized on the chart on the following page.

In the previous chapter of this book, we saw God move to restore many truths to the Church. We traced the restoration of –

SALVATION BY FAITH in the days of Luther,

WATER BAPTISM with men like Hubmaier,

HOLINESS with the Pietists and John Wesley,

HEALING through vessels like A.B. Simpson and,

The BAPTISM OF THE HOLY SPIRIT at the turn of the century.

But as you can see, the Church has not yet come to the ultimate in God's plan. The Church is not yet to the place of perfect manhood, *"unto the measure of the stature of the fulness of Christ (Ephesians 4:13).* Evidently there is more that   God desires for His people than we have experienced thus far, if we are to come to the sixth day experience -- the image of His Son.

As we move on from the early 1900's, we find that God has opened the doors of further truth, leading us a step further in His wonderful plan. In the late 1940's there was a renewed soberness among many Christians in conservative circles. They still felt that they had not experienced all that God had for them. They had experienced salvation by faith; they had been baptized; they were filled with the Spirit; but they still had a longing in their heart for more of God. They knew that there had to be more to the Christian walk than just getting filled with the Spirit. In several places in different parts of the world there went forth, as it were, the sound of a trumpet calling men together to a solemn assembly *(Numbers 10)*. Men responded to the wooing of the Spirit by gathering themselves

Restoration as Pictured in:

THE EARTH	MANKIND	THE CHURCH
1. The earth was created good from the hands of God (Isaiah 45:18, Genesis 1:1).	1. Man was created good from the hands of God (Genesis 1:26-27, 31).	1. The Early Church began in great power from its birth by the Spirit of God (Acts 2).
2. Some catastrophe marred this beautiful creation (Genesis 1:2).	2. Sin marred God's creation (Genesis 3).	2. The Church declined as man's will was given priority.
3. The earth was in a condition of darkness (Genesis 1:2).	3. Man in sin is dwelling in darkness (John 3:19).	3. The Church entered into what is called the "Dark Ages".
4. The Spirit of God began to move (Genesis 1:2).	4. The Spirit prepares the heart of man (1 Corinthians 12:3).	4. The Spirit of God moved on a man named Martin Luther.
FIRST DAY 5. There is a separation of light from darkness (Genesis 1:3-5).	5. In SALVATION man is brought from darkness to light (Matthew 4:16; I Peter 2:9).	5. Justification by faith is restored to the Church, and the two Kingdoms are established.
SECOND DAY 6. A Separation of the waters occurs (Genesis 1:6-8).	6. A separation is effected in WATER BAPTISM (Romans 6:3-4).	6. Water Baptism is restored through the Anabaptists.
THIRD DAY 7. The dry ground springs from the sea, and the kind bring forth fruit (Genesis 1:9-13).	7. Resurrection to newness of life and fruitfulness follow Water Baptism (Romans 6:4; 7:4).	7. God brings emphasis of holy living and fruitfulness through men like Wesley.
FOURTH DAY 8. Here we find an emphasis on the rulership and government of the light (Genesis 1:14-19).	8. The BAPTISM OF THE HOLY SPIRIT helps establish God's government and rulership over us.	8. The Spirit is again able to control the Church that has experienced this Spirit baptism.
FIFTH DAY 9. The first mention of life in the Bible is associated with the word "abundantly" (Genesis 1:20-23).	9. Now the believer is in the position to experience life "more abundantly" (John 10:10).	9. The Church experiences some of the abundant riches in Christ — body unity, health and life.
SIXTH DAY 10. Man is created in the image of God (Genesis 1:24-31).	10. Every man in Christ is to come to the image of His Son (Romans 8:29-30).	10. The Church is to experience a Day of Atonement in the Feast of Tabernacles (Ephesians 4:13).
SEVENTH DAY 11. After finishing, blessing and sanctifying His work, God rested (Genesis 2:1-3).	11. Each believer can have a place of rest in the will and plan of God (Hebrews 4:9-11).	11. The Church will one day experience rest.

together in fasting, prayer and seeking the face of God.

Prayer waters revival and visitation. As the vapours of prayer ascended in the form of spiritual incense *(Revelation 5:8),* they formed bright clouds overhead *(Job 36:26-29; Zechariah 10:1),* and rain fell upon these open vessels. There are set times for God's rain to water the earth. Elias was a man who knew how to pray for rain in the time of rain *(James 5: 17-18).* God, who is the good husbandman, desires that there be rain on the earth *(James 5:7),* but there is a set time for the rain. We need to discern God's time. These men apparently did, for as the vapours went up, God rained upon them abundantly.

> *Job 36:27-28 - "For He maketh small the drops of water: they pour down rain according to the vapour thereof: which the clouds do drop and distil upon men abundantly."*

> *Zechariah 10:1 - "Ask ye of the Lord rain in the time of the latter rain; so the Lord shall make bright clouds, and give them showers of rain, to every one grass in the field."*

30. HOW DID GOD SPEAK IN THE LATE 1940's?

As men waited before the Lord, there was a sovereign outpouring of the Spirit on some of these that were waiting before Him. Men began to arise and prophesy with a powerful anointing of the Spirit. They prophesied about things that were contrary to their own doctrinal beliefs. They prophesied about the five ascension gift ministries, a further unfolding of the gifts of the Spirit and truths regarding body ministry; but the most pronounced message was in connection with THE LAYING ON OF HANDS.

These doctrines were new to their experience. They formerly believed none of these things, so they were forced to look to the Word of God. Ultimately the Word must be the final test of any and every doctrine. As they studied the Word to see what God has revealed in these areas, God removed the scales from their eyes, and the Word became alive.

After discovering the Word basis for what had been prophesied, these men began to move in the areas that had been indicated by the Spirit. As they met together, the Spirit continued to flow and open more areas of truth. The Presence of the Lord was so real that no human leader was needed in the services, and yet there was tremendous order. As men entered into God's Presence, audible praise began to flow from their lips in such a way as none had ever experienced.

31. WHAT BECAME OF THIS MOVEMENT OF GOD?

As God by His Spirit opened some powerful doors to these men, stern warnings came forth in prophecy. God indicated that they were only to operate in these realms as the Spirit directed. If they disobeyed, the move would go into religious chaos. This is precisely what happened. Although not everyone who was involved in this visitation disobeyed, many of these who were involved abused and misused the gifts that God gave them. These groups indeed ended in chaos. The truths were right, but they were corrupted by men.

There were those, however, who saw what was happening and took due warning. These preserved the truth as God had given it to them. Unfortunately, the movement was judged on the basis of the most radical element which used the gifts and callings of God for their own gain. Hence, many have looked with consternation on what took place in those years, letting the abuses and fanaticism of a few blind them to the spiritual truth God wanted to reveal.

It is unfortunate that men always judge a movement on the basis of the most radical example of that movement. Luther very likely judged the Anabaptists on the basis of what he knew about one man who was an Anabaptist. A fanatic named Melchior Hoffmann was an Anabaptist who proclaimed himself as the "apostle of the end". He predicted that the last judgment would come in 1533. Because this man was an Anabaptist, many people figured that all Anabaptists must be like him. We know this is not at all true.

A similar thing happened in the days of early Pentecostalism. God definately spoke to His people in those days. There were those who carried the truth into extreme emotionalism attracting attention to themselves. They carried on in all sorts of strange ways. They were characterized by displays of a variety of unscriptural manifestations. Because of the fanaticism of these unscriptural few, the whole movement was judged as being a fleshy, fanatical display of sheer emotionalism. Those who stood on the outside only saw those who abused the truth, and they wanted no part of Pentecostalism.

This, then, is precisely what happened in the early 1950's. Many who were involved in this original move went into extreme fanaticism and religious racketeering. Hence, the whole movement was considered negatively. It is extremely unfortunate that God's people miss out on experiences that God wants every believer to experience because they misjudge a true move of the Spirit of God. Satan will do his best to see that we are discouraged from entering into the fulness of our inheritance in Christ. In every genuine move of God Satan has sought to pervert what God was doing to make the truth unpalatable to the true people of God. This same thing has happened in nearly every visitation. Luther gave birth to fanatics like Karlstadt. Hubmaier gave birth to men like Hoffmann. But through it all, the truth that God revealed was a truth for the Body of Christ. In every case, however, Satan has succeeded in discouraging some of Christendom from accepting and receiving the PRESENT TRUTH.

32. WHAT ARE SOME OF THE TRUTHS THAT CAME OUT OF THIS VISITATION?

The central truth that was unlocked in this visitation was the laying on of hands. But, as men pursued after the hidden treasures in the Word of God with a renewed zeal, God began to unfold more and more of His ultimate purpose. The remainder of this book will be dealing with areas of truth that have opened since that outpouring about twenty-five years ago. Some of these truths include the following:

a)   The Restoration of the Lost Years.
b)   The Restoration of Full Fruit and the Gifts of the Spirit.
c)   The Laying on of Hands.
d)   The Revelation of the Body of Christ.
e)   The Five Ascension Gift Ministries.
f)   The Principles of Church Order and Government.
g)   Worship in Spirit and in Truth.
h)   The Tabernacle of David.
i)   The Seven Principles of the Doctrine of Christ. *(Hebrews 6:1-2).*
j)   The Maturity of the Saints.

All former visitations dealt chiefly with the relation of the believer to God as an individual. They included an emphasis on man's personal salvation, his personal death and burial in baptism, his personal walk, his personal health and his personal reception of the Holy Spirit. This move, however, is on a different level. The areas that have been illuminated by the Spirit in the present move all have to do with the corporate Body of Christ. The trumpet call that sounded was a call for the gathering together of the Body—a call to oneness or spiritual unity. It is this Body or Man which God is building or fashioning that is to be conformed to the IMAGE. It is this many-membered man *(I Corinthians 12).*

33.   WHAT IS THE DOCTRINE OF THE LAYING ON OF HANDS?

A good definition of a doctrine is "the sum of all scripture passages on a given subject." While we will not attempt to cite all the scripture references on the subject of hands or the laying on of hands, it is essential that we outline some of the more important scriptures relating to this important study (Note: The reader is encouraged to do a concordance study in this area).

a)   Hands in the scripture are often connected with natural and spiritual power.

Leviticus 9:22 - "And Aaron lifted up his hand toward the people, and blessed them, and came down from offering of the sin offering, and the burnt offering, and peace offerings" (Connect Luke 24:50).

II Samuel 20:21 - ". . . But a man of Mount Ephraim, Sheba. . . hath lifted up his hand against the king, even against David."

Psalm 20:6 - "Now know I that the Lord saveth his anointed; He will hear him from His holy heaven with the saving strength of His right hand."

Isaiah 41:10 - "Fear thou not; for I am with thee: be not dismayed; for I am thy God: I will strengthen thee; yea, I will help thee; yea, I will uphold thee with the right hand of My righteousness."

b)   The laying on of hands in the Old Testament.

1)   Jacob CONFERRED A BLESSING on Joseph's sons by the laying on of hands. It is interesting to note that a greater blessing was conferred through the right hand of Jacob. This was not just a form, but there was something powerful taking place here.

Genesis 48:14-16 - "And Israel stretched out his right hand, and laid it upon Ephraim's head, who was the younger, and his left hand upon Manasseh's head, guiding his hands wittingly; for Manasseh was the firstborn. And he blessed Joseph, and said, God, before whom my fathers Abraham and Isaac did walk, the God which fed me all my life long unto this day, the Angel which redeemed me from all evil, bless the lads; and let my name be named on them, and the name of my fathers Abraham and Isaac; and let them grow into a multitude in the midst of the earth."

2) Under the Levitical system, the priests were instructed often times to lay hands upon the animal that was to be offered to the Lord. In some cases they were to confess their sins as they laid hands on the animal. In so doing, there was a typical TRANSMISSION of guilt from the man to the sacrifice.

Leviticus 16:21-22 - "And Aaron shall lay both his hands upon the head of the live goat, and confess over him all the iniquities of the children of Israel, and all their transgressions in all their sins, putting them upon the head of the goat, and shall send him away by the hand of a fit man into the wilderness: and the goat shall bear upon him all their iniquities unto a land not inhabited: and he shall let go the goat in the wilderness."

See also: Exodus 29:10; Leviticus 1:4,8,13; 14:15, 24,33; 8:14.

3) Witnesses against a criminal often laid their hands on the head of the accused before stoning him. In this way they made a CONFIRMATION of their witness or testimony against him.

Leviticus 24:14 - "Bring forth him that hath cursed without the camp; and let all that heard him lay their hands upon his head, and let the congregation stone him."

See also: Deuteronomy 17:7.

4)   God had chosen the Levites to serve before Him as priests. These were actually chosen as a substitute for all the firstborn of Israel. When the Levites were consecrated or OR-DAINED, the children of Israel laid their hands on them making the TRANSFERENCE of this authority valid.

Numbers 8:9-11 - "And thou shalt bring the Levites before the tabernacle of the congregation: and thou shalt gather the whole assembly of the children of Israel together: and thou shalt bring the Levites before the Lord: and the children of Israel shall put their hands upon the Levites: and Aaron shall offer the Levites before the Lord for an offering of the children of Israel, that they may execute the service of the Lord."

5)   When God desired a man to take Moses' place, He singled out Joshua. Joshua was the Lord's choice, not the choice of Moses. Yet it was Moses who laid his hands upon Joshua. In doing so he ORDAINED Joshua for this call-ing, he IMPARTED to him the necessary gift (wisdom) for the task, he ACKNOWLEDGED Joshua's Divine appointment and he TRANS-FERRED spiritual power unto him *(Numbers 27:15-23).*

Deuteronomy 34:9 - "And Joshua the son of Nun was full of the spirit of wisdom; for Moses had laid his hands upon him: and the children of Israel harkened unto him, and did as the Lord commanded Moses.''

c) The laying on of hands in the New Testament.

1) The laying on of hands is often used in the New Testament in connection with HEALING.

a) Jesus used the laying on of hands extensively in His healing ministry.

Luke 4:40 - ''Now when the sun was setting, all they that had any sick with divers diseases brought them unto Him; and He laid His hands on every one of them, and healed them.''

See also: Matthew 8:3, 15; 9:29; Mark 1:41; 5:23; 6:5; 7:32; 8:23; 16:18; Luke 5:13; 13:13; 22:51.

b) The disciples also extended this ministry of healing by the laying on of hands.

Acts 5:12 - ''And by the hands of the apostles were many signs and wonders wrought among the people; (and they were all with one accord in Solomon's porch. . .).

See also: Acts 9:17; 14:3.

c) Paul also laid his hands on the sick, and they were healed!

Acts 28:8 - ''And it came to pass, that the father of Publius lay sick of a fever and of a bloody flux: to whom Paul entered in, and prayed, and laid his hands on him, and healed him.'' *See also: Acts 19:11.*

d)   The Church today is to continue in the
impartation of Divine healing through the
hands. It is believers who make up the
Body of Christ, and we are to be His
hands extended.

*Mark 16:18 - "They (believers) shall lay hands
on the sick, and they (the sick) shall recover."*

2)   The laying on of hands can be seen in connection with the CONFERRING OF THE
HOLY GHOST. There are five cases of men or
companies receiving the Baptism of the Holy
Ghost in the Book of Acts, and three of these
definately mention the laying on of hands in
connection with the reception of this gift *(See
also Acts 9:17 and 19:6).*

*Acts 8:18 - "And when Simon saw that through
the laying on of the apostle's hands the Holy
Ghost was given, he offered them money. . ."*

3)   The laying on of hands was used in connection
with THE IMPARTATION OF SPIRITUAL
GIFTS. This is much like the Old Testament
case of Joshua receiving an impartation of wisdom from the hands of Moses. This impartation is to work in establishing and equipping
ministries *(Romans 1:11-12).*

*II Timothy 1:6, 14 - "Wherefore I put thee in
remembrance that thou stir up the gift of
God, which is in thee by the putting on of my
hands. . . that good thing which was committed
unto thee keep by the Holy Ghost which dwell-
eth in us."   See also: I Timothy 4:14.*

4) The laying on of hands is often ACCOMPAN-
IED BY PROPHECY.

*I Timothy 4:14 - "Neglect not the gift that is in thee,
which was given thee by prophecy, with the laying
on of hands of the presbytery."*

See also: I Timothy 1:18.

5) The laying on of hands was used in connect-
tion with THE IMPARTATION OF A BLES-
SING.

*Mark 10:16 - "And He took them up in His arms,
put His hands upon them, and blessed them."*

6) The laying on of hands was used in THE SEND-
ING OUT OF MINISTRIES. Perhaps there was
a CORPORATE IDENTIFICATION of the
Body with those who were being sent out.
They knew they were not going alone, but a
body was identified with them and would be,
in effect, going with them.

*Acts 13:2-3 - "As they ministered to the Lord, and
fasted, the Holy Ghost said, Separate me Barnabas
and Saul for the work whereunto I have called them.
And when they had fasted and prayed, and laid
their hands on them, they sent them away."*

7) The laying on of hands was used in connection
with THE CONFIRMATION OR ORDINA-
TION OF MINISTRIES .

*Acts 6:6 - "(The deacons) Whom they set before the
apostles: and when they had prayed, they laid their
hands on them."*

8)   There are several CAUTIONS that are found in regard to the ministry of the laying on of hands.

    a)   This is not something to be taken lightly or done suddenly. Because the act of laying on of hands is more than a mere outward symbol, and there is in fact an impartation to and an identification with the candidate, we must be very cautious in our use of this ministry.

    I Timothy 5:22 - "Lay hands suddenly on no man, neither be partaker of other men's sins: keep thyself pure."

    Amplified Bible reads: "Do not be in a hurry in the laying on of hands – giving the sanction of the church too hastily (in reinstating expelled offenders or in ordination in questionable cases) – nor share or participate in another man's sins; keep yourself pure."

    b)   In every case except in regard to healing, it was always the leadership who laid hands on the people. Perhaps because of the serious nature of many of these things, the novice is excluded from operating in such ministry.

34. WHAT IS THE IMPORTANCE OF THE LAYING ON OF HANDS FOR THE CHURCH TODAY?

We can expect that all of these uses of the laying on of hands found in the New Testament will find a place in the Church today. It is important for us to maintain a scriptural pattern in all we do, even if we do not understand the full significance of it. Just the fact that this ordinance was important in the functioning of the Early Church should make it important for us in the Church of this present day. This doctrine involves a supernatural impartation from generation to generation that is provided for us in no other aspect of church life. The church of this day should be using the laying on of hands. . .

a)   in praying for the sick,
b)   in the conferring of the Holy Ghost,
c)   in the impartation of spiritual gifts,
d)   in connection with prophecy to give confirmation and guidance,
e)   in the bestowing of a spiritual blessing,
f)   in the confirmation and ordination of ministries, and
g)   in the sending out of ministries from the Body.

As the Church of Jesus Christ begins to partake of some of the rich inheritance that has been given us in Christ, we will begin to use the tools that God has given us, we will see new hope for accomplishing the mission of the Church. God has not given us an impossible command, but the only way the commission will be realized is as we use the equipment that God has provided for the task. The weapons of our warfare are not carnal, but they are mighty! God is concerned that we war a good warfare (I Timothy 1:18).

STUDY QUESTIONS FOR CHAPTER FIVE

1. In what way does the account in *Genesis 1* typify what God is doing in restoration?

2. What is the most prominent message of the present visitation?

3. On what basis have many of the visitations of the past been judged?

4. How was the laying on of hands used in the Old Testament?

5. List seven ways in which the laying on of hands was used in the New Testament?

6. What cautions does the Scripture give us in regard to the use of the laying on of hands?

7. Why do we need the laying on of hands in the Church today?

CHAPTER SIX

God's Principle Of Authority And Covering

God's Principle
Of Authority
And Covering
Chapter Six

God is moving in this present day in a marvelous way. If we had to single out one key that is foundational to what God is doing in the present day, we would have to say that God is restoring an awareness of and an appreciation for the Body of Christ. The laying on of hands, which we discussed in the previous chapter, is only possible because of a renewed relationship in the Body of Christ. An understanding of the Body of Christ, however, necessitates an understanding of God's principle of authority and covering given us by Paul in *I Corinthians.*

> *I Corinthians 11:3 - "But I would have you know, that the head of every man is Christ; and the head of the woman is the man; and the head of Christ is God."*

In this verse we have an implication that is contained all throughout the Scripture, that God the Father is the ultimate figure in the Godhead. Before we come to know the Lord, we are drawn or moved upon by the Holy Spirit *(I Corinthians 12:3).* It is the ministry of the Holy Spirit to point us or lead us to Christ and to bear witness of Him *(John 5: 31-32; 15:26).* But this is not the ultimate in God's plan. It is the ministry of Christ, then, to bring us to perfect fellowship with the Father *(I Corinthians 15:28).*

In prophesying of the last days, Jesus said, *"Take heed that no man deceive you." (Matthew 24:4).* We are living in days in which it is crucial that God's people be properly re-

lated to godly leaders who will not lead them astray. We must
know those in authority over us and allow God to "cover"
our lives through their ministry.

But how is all this going to be realized? How are the purposes of God going to be accomplished? The only way any of
this plan can be realized in our experience is through submission to God's chain of authority. In this chapter we want to
examine the area of authority and headship in relation to the
Church, the Body of Christ.

35. WHAT IS GOD'S PURPOSE IN PICTURING THE CHURCH AS THE BODY OF CHRIST?

Whenever God gives us a further revelation of the Church
of Jesus Christ, He does so to emphasize another facet of
this tremendous organism. There is no one picture that
can adequately describe what God has in mind for His
people. So Paul relates the Church to A TEMPLE that
we might see God's intention of building a people together for an habitation of God by the Spirit *(Ephesians 2:
20-22)*. He pictures the Church as A FAMILY that we
might appreciate God's purpose in making us joint heirs
with our elder brother, the Lord Jesus Christ *(Hebrews
2:10, 14-17; Romans 8:17)*. He compares the Church to
A BRIDE that we might understand the oneness that
Christ and His Church are to experience *(Genesis 2:24;
John 17:11, 21)*.

What is God's purpose in giving us the revelation of THE
BODY of Christ? Simply this, God wants us to understand
Christ's desire to use His present Body, the Church, to minister
life and healing in the same way that He ministered in His
earthly walk *(I Corinthians 12:1-31)*. This is a tremendously
high calling, which demands a body of people who are functioning in the same realms of power and authority in which
Christ ministered. Before man can ever be entrusted with such

power and authority, there must be a recognition of the Divine principles of headship and a submission to Christ, the Head of the Body.

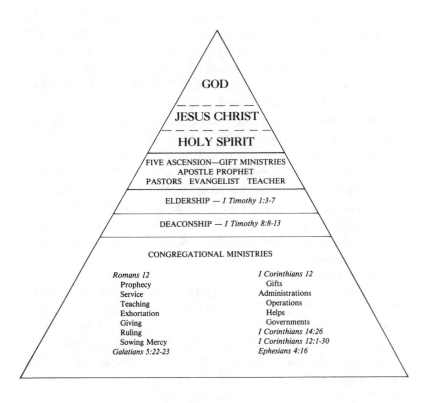

GOD

JESUS CHRIST

HOLY SPIRIT

FIVE ASCENSION—GIFT MINISTRIES
APOSTLE PROPHET
PASTORS   EVANGELIST   TEACHER

ELDERSHIP — *I Timothy 1:3-7*

DEACONSHIP — *I Timothy 8:8-13*

CONGREGATIONAL MINISTRIES

Romans 12
Prophecy
Service
Teaching
Exhortation
Giving
Ruling
Sowing Mercy
Galatians 5:22-23

I Corinthians 12
Gifts
Administrations
Operations
Helps
Governments
I Corinthians 14:26
I Corinthians 12:1-30
Ephesians 4:16

36. WHAT DO WE MEAN THAT CHRIST IS THE HEAD OF THE BODY?

Paul clearly tells us that the Church is Christ's Body and that Christ Himself is the Head over this Body *(Ephesians 1:22-23).* To get a better picture of Christ's relationship to the Church, we merely have to look at our natural body and see the natural relationship between our head and our physical body.

In the natural being, the head is the home of the brain, that intricate organism which through energy impulses is able to command and control the members of the body. In order for the natural body to function properly, it must respond positively to all of the impulses sent from the head. Failure on the part of the body to respond properly to the head's directions results in spasticated movements. In this condition the body can accomplish a certain measure of work, but it will not be of the quality or the quantity that could be possible if every member was functioning properly. Failure on the part of the body to respond at all to the impulses from the head indicates that the nerve involved has been severed or deadened. In either case, it is cut off from its source. No arm has the capability of thinking for itself. When nerves are severed it results in paralysis. If the entire head is severed from the body, it will bring death in every case.

Just as the head relates to the natural body, so Christ is to relate to the Church, His Body. He is to give instructions and directions to the Church which is to respond positively to those directives. As the Head, He sends impulses by way of the Holy Spirit to the Body, and the Body is to respond to whatever the Head has commanded. To be cut off from the Head is to be cut off from the source of life. In every case it will bring spiritual death.

As we have already seen, God has a chain of command. God's chain of command relates to all three of the divinely ordained institutions. There is a chain of command in

37. WHAT IS THE SCRIPTURAL PRINCIPLE OF HEAD-SHIP?

the government. God has ordained the powers that are in rule. He sets the kings on their thrones *(Daniel 2:21)*, and they are accountable to God for their stewardship of these trusts *(Luke 16:2)*. The government has its heirarchy or chain of command, but God is the head of all things. When everyone is properly submitted to the authority placed over them, they are all under the shadow of the Almighty, under the wings of His protection and covered against all storms. Let anyone step out from under his proper headship, and he steps out from under the cloud.

God's Chain of Command in the Government

The family is another institution that is ordained of God. The family has its chain of command also. The husband is under God, the wife is under the husband, and the wife is called along side to be a partaker of the husband's headship over the children. Again, every member is responsible to the head that is over him.

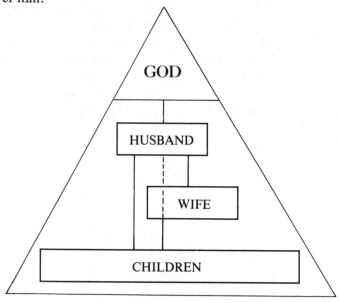

God's Chain of Command in the Family

The Church, the third institution ordained of God, is no different. It, too, has a proper chain of command. God the head of all things gave to His Son headship over the Church *(Ephesians 1:20-23)*. Christ now functions in His Body through the ministry of the Holy Spirit *(John 14:18, 26)*. God has given authority to overseers to administer this headship over the Church.

All three of these models have the same headship. All three of these institutions are under the headship of God. But each member as he finds his place in these models has one or more heads over him. To this head over him there must be submission if that individual is to find fulfillment in God's plan and purpose. To this head there must be submission if that individual is to find a place of safety under the shadow of the Almighty.

When we fully understand this principle of headship, we see that all the power and authority is in the Head. Apart from the Head, there is no authority. The Head is the source of all authority; all other authority is delegated authority. AS WE SUBJECT OURSELVES TO THE HEAD THAT IS OVER US, WE BECOME PARTAKERS OF HIS POWER AND AUTHORITY, or we become candidates for the channeling of God's power.

To exemplify this principle, let us examine the life of Jesus. We know when Jesus became flesh, He laid aside His prerogative to act as God. He emptied Himself, and He became obedient *(Philippians 2:5-8)*. Jesus gave up all His rights into the hands of the Father and completely subjected Himself to the will, plan and purpose of the Father *(John 4:34; 5:30; 6:38; 15:10)*. As Jesus subjected Himself to the Father, the Father bestowed upon Him great power. We know, for example, when His testing was finished that He came forth in the power of the Spirit of God *(Luke 4:14)*. As Jesus submitted Himself to the authority of the Father, the Father in turn gave to Him authority or made Christ to be a partaker of His authority. He actually made Christ a steward of His power and authority.

As Jesus walked on the earth in perfect obedience to the Father, He was a living demonstration of the power of God—not His own power, but power and authority that had been entrusted to Him by the Father. So we see Jesus exercising the power to forgive sins *(Matthew 9:6)*. He is given power and authority over devils, disease and the elements of nature *(Matthew 8:1-17, 23-27)*. Because of Christ's faithfulness, God entrusted Him with great power.

Jesus partook of the power of the Father in His earthly walk. In His ministry He chose twelve disciples to minister with Him. The disciples, under the headship of Christ, also became partakers of this power as they were properly submitted to Christ their head. They, too, were able to go forth with authority, but it was only as they were properly submitted *(Luke 9:1-2; 10:1, 9, 17)*.

This principle of headship is the same principle that works in the armed forces. All of the power and authority is in the Commander-in-Chief. When the Commander-in-Chief looks for instruments or channels to carry out his purposes, he looks for those who are properly submitted to him. How does a person demonstrate his submission? He demonstrates submission by obeying the one who is over him. When the Commander finds obedient and loyal subjects, he gathers them around him as his Generals and bestows great power and authority upon them, making them partakers of His power and authority. Now the General is able to give orders and commands that carry the same force as if they came directly from the Commander-in-Chief. As long as the General remains properly submitted, this will always be the case. He will always speak with the authority of the head.

In the armed forces there are various ranks, and each man has his charge (those that are under him) and his head (those that are over him). If he is properly submitted to his head, he has authority over his charge because he is a partaker of the authority of the head. As the Sergeant submits to the Lieutenant, he becomes a partaker of the authority, not of the Lieutenant himself, but of the power with which the Lieutenant has been entrusted. All the actual power is in the head; there are only various stewards of this same power.

This same principle must apply in all three institutions ordained of God—the government, the family and the Church. When Jesus rose from the dead, God entrusted Him with great power *(Matthew 28:18; Romans 14:9)*. But when Jesus ascended on high, He was exalted at the right hand of God and given to be Head over the Church *(Ephesians 1:20-23)*.

Matthew 26:64 - "Jesus saith unto him, Thou hast said: nevertheless I say unto you, hereafter shall ye see the Son of man sitting on THE RIGHT HAND OF POWER, and coming in the clouds of heaven."

Colossians 2:10 - "And ye are complete in Him, which is THE HEAD OF ALL PRINCIPALITY AND POWER."

I Peter 3:22 - "Who is gone into heaven, and is on the right hand of God; angels and authorities and powers BEING MADE SUBJECT UNTO HIM."

We see that Jesus at the present time has all things in His hands. He now desires to function through the Church, His Body, in the same way that the Father functioned through Him. Even as Jesus mirrored the Father, we are to mirror Christ. In order for this to happen, it means that we are going to have to submit fully to the headship of Christ. To submit to his headship implies a life of complete obedience to His commands, *"If ye love Me, keep my commandments" (John 14:15).* As we subject ourselves to the headship of Jesus Christ, He will bestow on us great power, but we must be in a place of submission *(Mark 16:15-20)!* As the Church subjects itself to Christ, it will have all things under its feet, for we will be partakers of the power that is Christ's.

STUDY QUESTIONS FOR CHAPTER SIX

1. What is God's purpose in giving us the revelation of the Body of Christ?

2. In what respect is Christ to be the Head of the Body?

3. What is the chain of command in the government?

4. What is the chain of command in the family?

5. What is the chain of command in the Church?

6. How does one qualify to become a partaker of authority and power of the Head?

CHAPTER
SEVEN

*Order And Government
In The Church*

Order And Government In The Church

Chapter Seven

In the previous chapter we examined the chain of command in the three God-given institutions, the civil government, the family and the Church. Satan, in these last days, is seeking to destroy all three of these institutions through rebellion and iniquity. These are days that are characterized by rebellion and revolution against the ruling authorities of every sphere. The authority of the father in the home is being undermined by much teaching in regard to permissiveness. The authority of the Church is being questioned by the liberal thinkers of the day. These are days of street demonstrations, riots, campus upheavals, revolution and chaos; not just in America, but in every country of the world.

What a contrast this is to the life of Jesus. Jesus obeyed the laws of the land, even recognizing the foreign government control paying tribute when it was due. He taught respect and obedience to those in authority. He preached about the condition of man's heart; and He knew if this message was heeded, it would bring restoration to all areas of society. Jesus' teaching is carried over by the apostles of the Early Church. They also taught obedience to the civil government.

Romans 13:1-4 "Let every soul be subject unto the higher powers. For there is no power but of God: the powers that be are ordained of God. Whosoever therefore resisteth the power, resisteth the ordinance of God: and they that resist shall receive to themselves damnation. For rulers are not a terror to good works, but to the evil. Wilt thou then not be afraid of the power? do that which is good, and thou shalt have praise of the same: For he is a minister of God to thee for good. But if thou do that which is evil, be afraid; for he beareth not the sword in vain: for he is the minister of God, a revenger to execute wrath upon him that doeth evil."

They taught obedience in the home.

Ephesians 6:1-3 - "Children obey your parents in the Lord: for this is right. Honor thy father and mother; which is the first commandment with promise; that it may be well with thee, and thou mayest live long on the earth."

They taught obedience in the Church.

Hebrews 13:17 - "Obey them that have the rule over you, and submit yourselves: for they watch for your souls, as they that must give account, that they may do it with joy, and not with grief: for that is unprofitable for you."

Many Christians have no understanding of this important principle. They see the importance of obeying governmental officials; they acknowledge the necessity of having obedience in the home; but when it comes to the Church, they are not so eager to acknowledge human authority. Many acknowledge a desire to be submissive to the Holy Spirit as the ambassador of the rule of Christ in their life, but they don't see how this relates to submission to a physical Church or Body on earth. Many deceive themselves in thinking they are "led of the Spirit," when in reality they are rejecting God's chain of command in the Church and are eliminating themselves from divine guidance.

In studying the Scriptures relative to the Church, we cannot help but notice that the Godhead is involved in the headship of the Church (see diagram in previous chapter). The great plan and purpose of God through the ages has been to bring man back into full fellowship with Himself. The Godhead has been involved in this Plan of Redemption. The Father has had His particular ministry, the Son has had His role, and the Spirit is doing His work. They are all in complete unity moving toward a common goal. All of history is an unfolding of this Plan of Redemption. All of history can be divided into the work of the Father, the work of the Son and the work of the Spirit. As the three persons of the Godhead are co-equal, so are the divisions of history characterized by each.

THE WORK OF REDEMPTION

BEGINNING — All of History can be divided into Thirds — END

THE WORK OF THE	THE WORK OF THE	THE WORK OF THE
FATHER	SON	SPIRIT
2000 YEARS	Isaac Christar Offered Offered	2000 YEARS
Adam Abraham	2000 YEARS	Early Latter Rain Rain

The actual outworking of the Plan of Redemption did not commence until Adam had sinned. Sin broke God's rest and God's Plan of Redemption was under way. The work of the Father is seen particularly in the first 2000 years after the fall of man. This period of time extended from Adam, the father of the human race, up to Abraham, the father of all who believe *(Romans 4:11)*. In this period we have a manifestation of God's holiness and His hatred for sin (Flood). Yet inspite of judgment there is merciful kindness, for God loved the world and desired to save it *(I Peter 3:20, John 3:16)*. It is in this span of history that we see God making the covenant with Noah and an everlasting covenant with Abraham. The Father's burden was the WHOLE WORLD, and His gift to the world was His Son.

The second 2000 year period is characterized by the work of the Son. The Son's work did not begin with the incarnation, but His *"goings forth have been from of old, from everlasting" (Micah 5:2)*. Isn't it interesting that it is Abraham who encounters Melchizedek *(Genesis 14)*, King of Righteousness who was *"made like unto the Son of God"(Hebrews 7:3)*. It is with Abraham and the birth of his only begotten son, Isaac, that we begin to see a further unfolding of the Plan of Redemption. From this point on we have a heavy emphasis on the sacrificial blood that is to be shed for man's sin. God makes a covenant with Abraham that requires the shedding of blood (circumcision) and Abraham is instructed to sacrifice his only begotten son. This period begins, then, with the typical sacrifice of the only begotten son, Isaac, and culminates in the sacrifice of THE only begotten Son of God on Calvary. The burden of the Son was the providing of a wife for Himself. Even as Adam's wife came from his side *(Genesis 2:22)*, so also Christ's wife was to come from His side *(John 19:34)*. The burden of the Son was for a glorious Church. On Calvary, He made such a Church possible by shedding sinless blood for the redemption of sinful man. This provided for the Church, but this provision still needed to be appropriated by the Church.

Jesus' work was finished at Calvary in His death and resurrection. When He ascended, however, He sent the Holy Spirit to lead the Church into what He had provided. The next period of history involves the work of the Holy Spirit in the Church. This work began on the Day of Pentecost when the early rain dropped upon the expectant Church. This work of the Spirit will find its culmination at the end of the age preceeding the second coming of Christ when the Spirit will be poured out on all flesh *(Joel 2:28)*. It is at this season of harvest that we will receive the latter rain outpouring *(James 5:7)*. At the second coming of Christ this work or Plan of Redemption will be complete, restoration will have taken its course, and God will again rest.

As we have seen, the entire Godhead has been involved in the Plan of Redemption, but at the present time, the Holy Spirit is the one who is executing the plan. The Holy Spirit is the one who is transmitting directions from the Head to the Body. He is leading us into all truth *(John 16:13)* wherein we will be made free, free from sin *(John 8:32, 36)*. The Holy Spirit operates through various means to accomplish this plan and purpose. He uses the gifts and operations of the Spirit, but He also uses various ministries that have been given and set into the Body. He operates through a God-ordained chain of command. IF A PERSON DESIRES TO BE SUBMISSIVE TO THE HOLY SPIRIT, HE MUST SUBMIT TO THE CHANNELS OF AUTHORITY USED BY THE HOLY SPIRIT.

One thing that God has been teaching us in this present visitation is the necessity of the Local Church. It is essential for us to have an understanding of how the Holy Spirit works in and through this chosen channel. The Holy Spirit is accompanied by gifts, ministries and operations, but all of these must find their place of expression in connection with the Local

Church. No one person can minister alone. No one person has all he needs. No one person has all the gifts, ministries and operations functioning in his life, but the local body of believers should be complete, freely functioning in all areas. The Church is the proper setting for all of the gifts and operations of the Spirit to find their proper expression, for it is in this setting that God has provided leadership to guide, direct and to check the use of these gifts.

In this chapter we want to examine the leadership ministries that God has ordained for the Body of Christ, that His purposes might be accomplished. Hopefully we will see our need to not merely submit to the Holy Spirit, but to submit to God's chain of authority in the Church. For in so doing, we are, in fact, submitting to the Holy Spirit.

38. WHAT IS THE FIVE-FOLD MINISTRY GIVEN TO THE CHURCH BY CHRIST?

When Jesus ascended to the Father, He was not deserting the Church, He was providing for it. It was expedient for Jesus to leave, for as long as He remained on earth He was confined to a particular place. What Jesus wanted to do was world-wide. So He ascended to the right hand of the Father, took His position as Head over the Church and sent the Holy Spirit as He had promised. Now it was possible for Him, by the Spirit, to be present wherever two or three were gathered together *(Matthew 18:20)*. On the Day of Pentecost, the ascended Lord fulfilled His ministry as the Baptizer with the Holy Spirit *(Matthew 3:11)* and ignited the Church.

In addition to the Spirit, Christ also gave something else to the Church. God always uses human vessels to accomplish His purposes. Christ gave the Spirit to lead men into all truth, but the Spirit uses the instruments that Christ gave also. When Jesus ascended on high He gave the five-fold ministry to the church—apostles, prophets, evangelists, pastors and teachers.

> *Ephesians 4:8-11 - "Wherefore he saith, when He ascended up on high, He led captivity captive, and gave gifts unto men. (Now that He ascended, what is it but that He also descended first into the lower parts of the earth? He that descended is the same also that ascended up far above all heavens, that He might fill all things.) And he gave some, apostles; and some, prophets; and some, evangelists; and some, pastors and teachers. . ."*

These ministries were given by God and they are all necessary in order for the purposes of God to be fulfilled on the earth. One of the five is not enough. We need all of that which God has provided. Christ's desire is to have a glorious Church without spot or wrinkle *(Ephesians 5:27),* and He has provided the five-fold ministry to fulfill this ultimate plan in His people– *". . .until we all come to the unity of the faith."* *(Ephesians 4:13).* Until this purpose is accomplished, until we all come to the perfect man, we can expect these ministries to be important and functioning in the Church of Jesus Christ. They are not given only for a particular apostolic age, they are given to the Church, until such time as the Church measures up to the *"measure of the stature of the fulness of Christ"* *(Ephesians 4:13).*

> *Ephesians 4:12-16 - "For the perfecting of the saints, for the work of the ministry, for the edifying of the Body of Christ: till we all come in the unity of the faith, and of the knowledge of the Son of God, unto a perfect man, unto the measure of the stature of the fulness of Christ: that we henceforth be no more children, tossed to and fro, and carried about with every wind of doctrine, by the sleight of men, and cunning craftiness, whereby they lie in wait to deceive; but speaking the truth in love, may grow up into Him in all things, which is the Head, even Christ: from whom the whole Body fitly joined together and compacted by that which every joint supplieth, according to the effectual working in the measure of every part, maketh increase of the Body unto the edifying of itself in love."*

God's purpose will never be realized apart from this God-given government provided for the Church by Christ upon His ascension and exaltation.

39. WHAT IS THE MINISTRY AND FUNCTION OF EACH OF THESE FIVE MINISTRIES?

While it is not our purpose in this book to give a detailed analysis of each of these ministries (such a work would be a book in itself), we do feel obliged to give a simple definition of each.

a)   APOSTLE
       The word "apostle" literally means "one who is sent." This ministry is referred to many times throughout the New Testament. In fact, there are 81 references to apostles. There were the TWELVE Apostles, who undoubtedly have a special place in the Kingdom, having been intimately involved with the Lord and having been present at the foundation supper of the New Covenant *(Luke 22:14)*. But there were also other apostles as well who ministered in New Testament times. There were men like Andronicus *(Romans 16:7)*, Barnabas, Paul *(Acts 14:14)*, Titus *(II Corinthians 8: 23)*, Timothy *(I Thessalonians 1:1; 2:6)* and others. (Note: The Greek of *II Corinthians 8:23* for "messengers" is "apostoloi" from which we get "apostles."

The ministry of the apostles seems to be that of laying the foundations of Local Churches *(Ephesians 2:20)*. In doing so they are involved in establishing new assemblies *(I Corinthians 9:1-2)* and working with assemblies that are already established but in need of further grounding. Some of the signs of the New Testament apostolic ministry include the following:

1) He is characterized by humility (*I Corinthians 4:9; II Corinthians 10:18*).

2) He is sacrificial *(II Corinthians 11:22-23).*

3) His ministry is accompanied by signs and wonders *(II Corinthians 12:12).*

4) He is patient *(II Corinthians 12:12).*

5) He is set in the Body by God and not man *(I Corinthians 12:28).*

6) He does not lord it over the flock *(II Corinthians 1:24; I Peter 5:3).*

7) He must bear apostolic fruit *(I Corinthians 9: 1-2).*

b) PROPHET

The prophet is no new figure in the New Testament. Much like the prophets of old, they have a two-fold ministry of foretelling and forthtelling. That is, they foretell the future as God reveals it by His Spirit or they speak or bubble forth a word from God. The ministry of the prophet is most often coupled with the ministry of the apostle, and they are seen working together in foundational ministry *(Ephesians 2:20)*. Agabus is the most notable prophet in the book of Acts who foretells a famine and the imprisonment of Paul *(Acts 11:27-28; 21:10-14)*. Prophets are involved in ministry to the Body of Christ in assembly life *(I Corinthians 14:29-37);* in the ordaining and sending out of ministries under the auspices of the local assembly *(Acts 13:3);* and in exhortation, edification and comfort to the whole body *(I Corinthians 14:3).*

Some of the signs of a prophet include:

1) He must have the gift of prophecy
    (*I Corinthians 12:10).*

2)   He must be appointed by God *(I Corinthians 12: 28-29)*.

3)   He must exhibit a life of holiness and humility.

4)   He must be willing to have his prophecies judged *(I Corinthians 14:29)*.

c)   EVANGELIST

The word "evangelist" simply means "a proclaimer of good news." This word is used only three times in the New Testament. We are shown our need for an evangelist in the perfecting work in the Church. *(Ephesians 4:11)*; Paul instructs Timothy who was actually an apostle *(I Thessalonians 1:1)* to do the work of an evangelist *(II Timothy 4:5);* but if we want to know what the work of an evangelist is, we must look to the ministry of Philip, the evangelist *(Acts 21:8)*.

Philip's ministry is recorded for us in *Acts 8.* Here we must assume is a picture of the work of an evangelist. Philip seems to be involved in breaking new ground with the Gospel–with the message of salvation accompanied by healing and signs. His ministry is two-fold. He is involved in public evangelism *(Vs. 1-13),* and he is involved in personal evangelism *(Vs. 26-40).* In all his methods, however, he was very obedient to the Spirit of God, and he was conscious of his own limitations. He certainly did not feel that he was self-sufficient. The result of his work was the establishment of a Local Church.

d)   PASTORS

The word for "pastor" in the Greek is the same as the word "shepherd." Whereas the ministry of the apostles, prophets and evangelists seems to be of a mobile nature, the pastors are given to rule over local assemblies as the shepherds of God's local flock. Jesus was the Good Shepherd, and, hence, the true pattern for all shepherds. A true shepherd will. . .

1) Be a feeder of the sheep *(I Peter 5:2)*.
2) Be a guide to lead and govern the sheep *(I Peter 5:2)*.
3) Be a lover of the souls of the sheep *(Hebrews 13:17)*.
4) Care for the sheep *(John 10:13)*.
5) Be willing to lay down his life for the sheep *(John 10:15-18)*.
6) Be willing to defend the flock in times of trouble *(John 10:12)*.

e) **TEACHER**
Teachers are also essential to the perfecting of the saints. The gift ministry of the teacher involves much more than the expositions and explanations of the scriptures in the Bible class (All elders are to be able to teach), but this too is a ministry that must be patterned after Christ who was the Great Teacher. When Jesus taught, He taught *"as one having authority, and not as the scribes" (Matthew 7:29)*. The teaching ministry is that which builds the ediface on the foundation laid by the apostles and prophets. It is the teacher that is to give the saints deep roots. God's promise in these days is to restore true teachers to the Church *(Isaiah 30:20)*.

As we have already implied, Jesus Christ Himself is the pattern for all the five ministries. What we actually see Jesus doing as He ascends to the right hand of the Father is breaking down His ministry into five ministries and entrusting various vessels with a portion of His full ministry. In the Lord we see the fulness of all ministry. In this respect we can see Christ as – –

THE APOSTLE AND HIGH PRIEST *(Hebrews 3:1)*,
THE PROPHET *(John 4:19)*,
THE EVANGELIST *(Luke 4:18)*,
THE PASTOR OR SHEPHERD *(John 10:11)*,
THE TEACHER *(John 3:2)*.

All of these ministries are open to abuse by men. There are false apostles who are self-appointed, exploiting the people of God *(II Corinthians 11:13-15)*. There are false prophets who prophesy out of their own heart *(Acts 13:6)*. There are false evangelists who deceive the people of God with unscriptural methods and gimicks. There are false teachers who introduce "damnable heresies" *(II Peter 2:1)*. There are false pastors who are hirelings and love not the sheep and fleece the people of God *(Ezekiel 34:1)*. All through the Scripture there are stern warnings against such ministries. We have to be careful, however, that in seeing the false ministries we don't swing the other way and reject the true ministries that God HAS raised up in these areas. God wants to restore these ministries in their purity. We need to remain open to what God has for us. This area of the five-fold ministry is essential for us to understand if we are to come to the place God has purposed for us *(Ephesians 4:11-16)*. God has provided a way for us to test ministry. Let us, therefore, test ministry and not condemn all ministry on the basis of a fanatic we once heard of or knew personally.

> *Matthew 7:15-20 - "Beware of false prophets, which come to you in sheep's clothing, but inwardly they are ravening wolves. Ye shall know them by their fruits. Do men gather grapes of thorns, or figs of thistles? Even so every good tree bringeth forth good fruit; but a corrupt tree bringeth forth evil fruit. A good tree cannot bring forth evil fruit, neither can a corrupt tree bring forth good fruit. Every tree that bringeth not forth good fruit is hewn down, and cast into the fire. Wherefore by their fruits ye shall know them."*

40.   WHAT ARE THE OFFICES IN THE LOCAL CHURCH?

Although there are many ministries to be found in a normal New Testament Church, there are only two offices defined in the organization of the Local Church. These include the office of the deacon and the office of the elder. The elders are God's provision for the spiritual government of the Local Church. They take the oversight over God's flock *(I Timothy 3:1-7; Titus 1:5)*. Deacons are God's provision for oversight in the natural realms that must be part of every Local Church *(Acts 6:3-6; I Timothy 3:8-13)*.

41.   WHAT IS AN ELDER?

The word translated "elder" is the Greek word "presbuteros." This word simply means "senior" or "elderly." In the New Testament Church this term is particularly used to describe a man who is the opposite of a novice. Hence, the word "elder" is specifically descriptive of A MAN and not an office.

Two words that are commonly confused with the word "elder" are the words "bishop" and "pastor." When we see the New Testament relation of these words there is no need for confusion. The word "bishop" is a word that is descriptive of an office *(Acts 1:20)* or position which an elder receives. The word "pastor," which means shepherd or feeder, is descriptive of the work which an elder in the office of a bishop performs. To further illustrate this distinction notice the following Scripture verses in which these various terms are used (the literal rendering is provided in the brackets).

> *Acts 20:17,28 - "And from Miletus he sent to Ephesus, and called for the ELDERS of the Church. . .take heed therefore unto yourselves, and to all the flock, over the which the Holy Ghost hath made you overseers (BISHOPS), to feed (PASTOR) the church of God, which He hath purchased with His own blood."*

I Peter 5:1-2 - "The ELDERS which are among you I exhort. . .feed (PASTOR) the flock of God which is among you, taking the oversight (BISHOPRICK) thereof, not of constraint, but willingly; not for filthy lucre, but of a ready mind."

Titus 1:5-7 - ". . .that thou shouldest. . .ordain ELDERS in every city, as I had appointed thee. . .for a BISHOP must be blameless."

I Peter 2:25 - "For ye were as sheep going astray; but are now returned unto the Shepherd (PASTOR) and BISHOP of your souls."

Some today would have us believe that the bishop was of high rank and authority in the Early Church and is, therefore, evidence of the beginning of modern religious heirarchy. In doing this they are not being fair to the Scripture. On the contrary, there is no trace of an heirarchical authority in the Early Church. Each Local Church had its functioning ministries and its positions of authority, but no office is found which had authority over a multiple of Local Churches. There is evidence for the likelihood of a chief elder in any given local assembly, but his authority was only local. To this most Bible expositors heartily agree. The three words, "elder" or "presbyter," "bishop" and "pastor," are words describing the man, the office and the work, respectively. Shaff's BIBLE DICTIONARY makes this representative statement,

"In the N.T. term (BISHOP) is synonymous with presbyter or elder, with this difference--that bishop is borrowed from the Greek and signifies the function, presbyter is derived from an office in the synagogue and signified the dignity of the same office. These presbyters or bishops of the apostolic period were the regular teachers, pastors, preachers and leaders of the congregations."

To attempt to make some sort of organizational machinery out of these three words is certainly going beyond what the Scripture says. No elevation of one office over another is ever suggested in any way by these words.

42. WHAT IS THE WORK OF AN ELDER?

As we have already stated, it is the elder who has been ordained that is to take the oversight in the spiritual areas of the Church. In one sense anyone who has known the Lord for a long while is an elder, but to be involved in spiritual oversight, the elder must be ordained *(I Timothy 4:14; Titus 1:5).* In ordination there is an identification and recognition of ministers of the Word in the Local Churches. It is clear from the Scripture that the elder's main work and life are to center around one thing, and that is the Word of God. These are men who have been set apart unto the Gospel of God *(Romans 1:1),* and they are to make full proof of their ministry *(II Timothy 4:5).* This ministry around the Word of God is most essential if the Church is to be the ground and pillar of Truth.

The elders of a church are its pastors. We have already seen how these two terms are used interchangeably. Therefore we can conlude that the work of the elder is to pastor. "Pastor" comes from the same Greek word as the word "shepherd." The elder is to shepherd the flock. In so doing, his primary task will be to make sure that the sheep are properly fed, He will be a feeder of the flock. He will lead them into green pastures. In order to do this, the elder must have a solid personal relationship to the Word of God. This relationship to the Word of God could be enumerated as follows:

a)   The Word of God is committed to Him *(II Timothy 2:20.*

b)   They are to take heed to order their life around the Word *(I Timothy 4:16).*

c)   They are to give themselves wholly to the Word
      (I Timothy 4:15; Acts 6:2-4).
d)   They are to labor in the Word, *"treading out the
      corn" (I Timothy 5:18)*.
e)   They are to preach the Word *(II Timothy 4:2)*.

As a leader of the flock, however, his personal example
and moral life will be of utmost importance. Sheep are followers, and if they are to find the green pastures and the still
waters they must be led there. It is not enough for a shepherd
to tell the sheep where to go, he must go before them. His life
must be above reproach.

As a leader of God's flock he must have a personal relationship to the people. The sheep must know his voice, and he
must be able to call his sheep by name. He must not be a hire-
ling who cares not for the sheep but only uses them as a stepping stone to further advancement, stepping on the sheep.
This love relationship must be foundational if the shepherd is
to minister to the sheep in areas of teaching, reproving, rebuk-
ing, exhorting and guarding *(II Timothy 2-4)*. If he does not
love the sheep, the sheep will not respond.

43.   WHAT ARE THE QUALIFICATIONS FOR AN ELDER IN THE HOUSE OF GOD?

God is very particular about who ministers in His House.
Therefore, since it is His House, He wants to select those
that will rule over His House. In the economy of God no
one just decides to be a minister. Every workman in
God's House must be divinely called *(Romans 1:1)*,
for if a man is divinely called, he will also be divinely
equipped. It takes supernatural enablement to be a
New Testament minister. Without this God-given
equipment, no amount of preparation or schooling will
do any good toward making men ministers. In fact, it
does a great deal of harm when organizations ordain
men to the ministry who are not called and equipped by
God. Apart from being called and equipped by God,

however, there are lists of qualifications that are given us in the Word of God to which a minister must measure up. We find such lists in *I Timothy 3:1-7 and Titus 1: 5-9.* We should notice that the New Testament does not put these qualifications forth as an ideal to strive for, but they are listed as THE STANDARD for all elders. These are qualifications that all elders MUST have *(I Timothy 3:2)*. Let us examine these qualifications that include moral, domestic and spiritual areas.

a) MORAL QUALIFICATIONS - There are certain qualities of character that must be manifest in the life of every individual who would seek to lead the people of God. There are attributes of character that are necessary, and there are attributes that are not to be found in the life of such a candidate.

1) The elder is to be BLAMELESS *(I Timothy 3:2; Titus 1:6)*. This does not mean that he will not be blamed for things, but that he will not be guilty. Jesus was blameless and yet false witnesses blamed Him for many things.

2) An elder must be TEMPERATE *(I Timothy 3:2; Titus 1:8)*. In other words he must have his self under control, exhibiting self-control. To have self-control is to have the spirit under God's control.

3) An elder is to be SOBER *(I Timothy 3:2; Titus 1:8)*. The elder is to be a man of infinite discretion and a sound mind. He is one who has his mind trained or cultivated toward wisdom and sound judgment.

4) An elder must be of GOOD BEHAVIOR *(I Timothy 3:3)*. This Greek word implies the thought of being orderly and modest. It is closely akin to the word which means "adornment." The elder must be above reproach in all his activities of behavior, right down to the way he dresses. He is

continually in the public eye, and there will always be those who will seek to bring reproach to the man of God.

5) An elder is NOT to be GIVEN TO WINE *(I Timothy 3:3; Titus 1:7)*. This seems like a rather obvious qualification, but there are many ministries who have fallen over this very thing.

6) An elder is NOT to be A STRIKER *(I Timothy 3:3; Titus 1:7)*. An elder is a minister in spiritual battles and is not to be given to physical displays. A man who still needs to brawl is a man who has not yet given all his rights over to the Lord.

7) An elder is NOT to be GREEDY OF MONEY *(I Timothy 3:3; Titus 1:7)*. A man who has given himself wholly unto the Lord will have no need of extravagances. Money will never be the motivation for his decisions in life.

8) An elder is NOT to be A BRAWLER *(I Timothy 3:3; Titus 1:7)*. He is not to be contentious, quarrelsome or argumentative. Again, such a man has not yet yielded his members and rights totally unto God.

9) An elder is NOT COVETEOUS *(I Timothy 3:3)*. He is a man who has learned to be content in whatsoever state God has placed him. His desires are toward spiritual things and not temporal things *(I Corinthians 12:31)*.

10) An elder is NOT to be SELF-WILLED *(Titus 1:7)*. A man who insists on his own way is not open to God's way. A man who is self-willed is one "so far overvaluing any determination at which he has himself once arrived that he will not be removed from it" (Trench). The Greek word carries the connotation of one who is self-pleasing, dominated by self-interest and inconsiderate of others. It is the opposite of gentleness.

11) An elder is to be a LOVER OF GOOD *(Titus 1:8* - The word "men" is not found in the Greek.) An elder never has a good thing to say about any practice of evil because he has a Christ-like hatred for evil.

b) DOMESTIC QUALIFICATIONS - The elder not only has to have himself under control, but he must have his own home under control. If he cannot rule effectively in his own house, how can he qualify to rule in God's House?

1) An elder must be the HUSBAND OF ONE WIFE *(I Timothy 3:2; Titus 1:6)*. God has never condoned polygamy. If he is a man who divides his natural affections, he will also be prone to divide his spiritual affections and commit spiritual adultery.

2) An elder is to be HOSPITABLE *(I Timothy 3:2; Titus 1:3)*. If one would break this Greek word down it would be translated "a lover of strangers." The shepherd must be able to call his sheep by name. To do this he must not be afraid to get involved with them on a personal level and have them into his home.

3) An elder is to RULE HIS OWN HOUSE WELL, having his own children in subjection *(I Timothy 3:4)*, having faithful children not accused of riot or unruly *(Titus 1:6)*. What a terrible blight it is that pastors' children have often been the most unruly. The exhortation goes on, *"For if a man know not how to rule his own house, how shall he take care of the Church of God" (I Tim.3:5)*.

c) SPIRITUAL QUALIFICATIONS - The elder needs to have certain spiritual qualities if he is going to fulfill the ministry to which he has been called. It takes more than a good man and a good father, it takes a man divinely enabled and equipped.

1)   An elder must be ABLE TO TEACH *(I Timothy 3:2)*. This does not mean that every elder must be gifted as a teacher as described under the five-fold ministry, but every elder must be able to expound, proclaim, and communicate what God has done in his life relative to the Word of God. He must be able to communicate it in such a way that others will learn.

2)   An elder is NOT to be a NOVICE or young convert *(I Timothy 3:6)*. For an elder in the House of God spiritual age is more important than physical age. The man who is newly planted lacks essential experience to lead others in the good and perfect way.

3)   An elder must be of GOOD REPORT AMONG THE UNSAVED *(I Timothy 3:7)*. The Church has a vital ministry to the unsaved. It is essential that the Church has projected a good image to those outside the Church.

4)   An elder is to be JUST *(Titus 1:8)*. In the etymology of this Greek word we find that it originally was used of persons who observed the custom, rule and right, especially in the fulfillment of duties towards gods and men, and of things that were in accordance with right. In the New Testament it denotes right conduct judged whether by the Divine standard or according to human standards of what was right (Vine).

5)   An elder is to be HOLY *(Titus 1:8)*. The Greek word used here is not the same word that refers to the holiness of God but it has some of the following connotations: "That quality of holiness which is manifested in those who have regard equally to grace and truth," those that are "religiously right as opposed to what is unrighteous or polluted," "those that are. . .pure from evil con-

duct, and observant of God's will" (Vine - Compare *I Thessalonians 2:10).*

6)   An elder must HOLD FAST THE FAITHFUL WORD as he has been taught *(Titus 1:9, 10-14).* This not only speaks of the ministry of an elder, but it tells us that he must be personally established in the truth, not blown about by winds of doctrine.

7)   An elder must be ABLE TO EXHORT AND CONVINCE in sound doctrine *(Titus 1:9).* He must be able to bring the truth to bear on the everyday encounters with the people he meets. He is not just a source of academic information.

All of these qualities are necessary in the life of that man who would rule in the House of God. God desires faithful stewards. He wants to make men stewards of God *(Titus 1:7).* He wants to entrust men with the mysteries of the Kingdom. These are the standards God sets for such a ministry.

44.   HOW IS AN ELDER TRAINED FOR SERVICE IN THE HOUSE OF THE LORD?

Before we go any further we want to affirm that the Scripture must be the sole rule for faith and practice. The Scripture is the total revelation of God to man and is sufficient to bring man to a full expression of the purpose and plan of God. Since it is a complete revelation we can expect that it would speak to every subject of import in the functioning of the New Testament Church. While we can go to no specific passage where it gives all the details for the training of ministry, all throughout the New Testament we have implication as to how leadership was most likely trained.

It is significant that there is no mention of Bible Schools, training centers, colleges or seminaries in the New Testament. The Local Church is the only training center that the New Testament Church knew. The Local Church was responsible for training all their people in the things of God. The ministry potential of the local bodies was not sent to one central place or one special school to be educated, they were educated under the home ministries.

When a man is to be a minister he is called to that position by God Himself. From his very birth God is grooming him by his experiences to fulfill his calling. As the individual responds to the work of the Holy Spirit in his life he grows in the grace that God has given to him. The further he progresses the more God reveals His purpose to this individual. As this individual becomes totally involved on the local level his gift will make room for him *(Proverbs 18:16)* and he will be given more and more local responsibility. In these years of training the young ministry is learning obedience and submission to those who are over him in the Lord. It is during this period that the young ministry is proving his ministry at home *(II Timothy 4:5; Acts 11:26)*. As this ministry qualifies himself before his local elders, the day will come when he will be set apart and given authority.

The Local Church is the center for all training. The Local Church may do this in any number of ways. It may have a Bible training school. It may have special classes for those aspiring to ministry. But whatever the case, we have no scriptural authority for sending trainees out to a centralized school. There are many dangers in such an approach, but the greatest danger is that they step out from under the covering of God's chain of command. New Testament ministries are tutored by God's ministries and apprenticed to older ministers. This was God's method when the need was greatest and it is bound to work today *(II Timothy 2:1-2)*.

As young ministries begin to develop in the local assembly, they will be given more and more responsibility. As they are faithful in the smaller tasks that they are given, they will be given more demanding and more responsible tasks. We can expect as such a ministry continues to serve in God's House that he will soon come to meet all of the qualifications for eldership. All of this time the faithfulness and the responsiveness of this individual to the Word of God and the chain of command has been observed by those who are in positions of authority in his local body. All of this time the ministry of this individual is being proven. For the man who is called to be an elder, the day will come when the local leadership will ordain him to serve in that capacity.

Elders were never elected by the local congregation; they were appointed by the oversight of the Church. Elders were always appointed or ordained in the New Testament Church by foundational ministries and other elders *(Acts 14:23; Titus 1:5; Acts 20:28)*. Fasting and prayer were usually connected with the ordination and sending out of ministries *(Acts 14:23; 13:2-3)*. These ministries would gather around the candidate, lay their hands on them and pray for them *(Acts 13:3)*. At this time one could expect God to confirm the choice by the prophetic Word *(I Timothy 1:18-19)*. Whom God calls, He qualifies; who God qualifies, He sends!

45. DO SPIRITUAL LEADERS HAVE ANY RIGHT TO RULE OVER GOD'S HOUSE?

It should be apparent by this time that the Church functions through a God-ordained chain of command. Strictly speaking we have to say that the Church is not democratic, it is theocratic. It is ruled from Christ down, and not from the people up. Christ's rule comes to us in different ways depending on where we find ourselves in relation to this chain of command. God has set elders in the Church as watchmen who are to rule under His authority. Many passages refer to this ruling of local leadership. In *I Timothy 3:4-5* it compares this ruling relationship to the father of a family. The elder has been given the oversight, but he is accountable to God.

Romans 12:8 - "Or he that exhorteth, on exhortation: he that giveth, let him do it with simplicity; he that ruleth, with diligence; he that sheweth mercy, with cheerfulness."

I Timothy 5:17 - "Let the elders that rule well be

*counted worthy of double honor, especially they who
labor in the word and doctrine."*

The elder, however, is in a very fearful place. He has
been given much authority over the people of God, but he
must be extremely careful that he does not use it to his own
gain. He must be very careful that he is genuinely interested in
the welfare of the sheep. He must be very careful to take good
care of the sheep *(I Timothy 3:4-5).* He is not to rule as a lord
over the flock, over God's heritage, but he is to pattern himself
after Christ *(I Peter 5:3).* Christ was the Lord of all and yet He
humbled Himself and became the servant of all *(John 13).* The
elder that rules unjustly will be judged of God. *"For unto
whomsoever much is given, of him shall be much required"*
(Luke 12:48). God will not let these unfaithful stewards off
without severe judgment *(Ezekiel 34:8-10).*

But on the other hand, the leaders that rule well are
worthy of double honor. A laborer is worthy of his hire, and
this goes for the man of God as well. Every Church no matter
what the size should be aiming at the support of its eldership
so that they can give themselves totally to the care of the
flock.

46.   WHAT IS A DEACON?

The word "deacon" is derived from the Greek word
"diakonos" which means "minister" or "servant."
This word is translated in any number of ways in the
New Testament and refers to many different ministries.
We are particularly interested in the office of a deacon
as seen in *Acts 6.* We notice in *Acts 6* that because of
the growth of the Church there were many temporal
things that needed to be administered. At first, evidently, the apostles treid to do all of these things, but as
time went on they realized they were going to have to
appoint others to take care of some of these daily administrations. Seven men were selected for this ministry.
They took this responsibility off the apostles so that the

apostles could give themselves more fully to prayer and ministry of the Word. A modern deacon would be an individual of similar function administering many of the physical affairs of the Church.

47. WHAT ARE THE QUALIFICATIONS FOR A DEACON?

We might think that it is not too important what the character of the man is who delivers a bag of groceries to a widow. But God is deeply concerned about the character of anyone who ministers in His Name. The apostles wanted the best that was available for this ministry. They asked for men of honest report, full of the Holy Ghost and wisdom *(Acts 6:3)*. In addition to this there is a list of qualifications found in the Scriptures. We have the list in *I Timothy 3:8-10*.

a) MORAL QUALIFICATIONS
   1) A deacon is NOT to be DOUBLE TONGUED *(I Timothy 3:8)*. This would imply that he is not to be a gossip. One who has a double tongue is one who says one thing to one person and gives a different view of it to another.
   2) A deacon is NOT to be GIVEN TO WINE *(I Timothy 3:8)*.
   3) A deacon is NOT to be GREEDY OF MONEY *(I Timothy 3:8)*.
   4) A deacon is to be BLAMELESS *(I Timothy 3:10)*.
   5) A deacon is to be PROVED (not a novice) *(I Timothy 3:10)*.

b) DOMESTIC QUALIFICATIONS
   1) A deacon is to be the HUSBAND OF ONE WIFE *(I Timothy 3:12)*.
   2) A deacon is to RULE HIS OWN HOUSE WELL *(I Timothy 3:12)*.

c)   SPIRITUAL QUALIFICATIONS
1)   A deacon must be FULL OF THE HOLY GHOST
       (Acts 6:3)
2)   A deacon must be FULL OF WISDOM *(Acts 6:3).*
3)   A deacon must be GRAVE *(I Timothy 3:8).*
       They are to be such that they inspire reverance
       and awe.
4)   A deacon must HOLD THE MYSTERY OF
       FAITH IN A PURE CONSCIENCE *(I Timothy
       3:9).*

Most of these qualifications are similar to those that we
discussed more fully under the qualifications for elders. It is
interesting that before someone could even wait on tables in
the Early Church he had to be a proven ministry. This really
puts many modern churches to shame who are not at all concerned about the character of many of their workers, but will
accept any volunteer.

48.   WHAT ARE THE QUALIFICATIONS FOR A DEA-
         CONESS?

The qualifications for a deaconess are the same as they
are for a deacon with a few special instructions in the
domestic areas. Many people feel that *I Timothy 3:11*
is talking about the wives of the deacons. This may be
true but there is no way to be sure from the Greek, for
it simply reads, *"Let women in like manner be grave. . ."*
Whatever the case is, four qualifications are listed for
such a woman.

1)   A deaconess must be GRAVE or reverent *(I Tim-
       othy 3:11).* She must handle herself in such a way
       that she commands respect.
2)   A deaconess must NOT be SLANDEROUS *(I
       Timothy 3:11).* This involves those who are given
       *"to finding fault with the demeanour and con-
       duct of others, and spreading their innuendos and*

criticisms in the church" (Vine).

3) A deaconess must be SOBER *(I Timothy 3:11).* This means she is known for her sound mind and good judgment.

4) A deaconess must be FAITHFUL in all things *(I Timothy 3:11).*

Note: Phoebe is an example of such a deaconess *(Romans 16: 1-5a).*

49. HOW ARE THE DEACONS APPOINTED IN THE LOCAL CHURCH?

We only have one case in scripture where deacons were set into a body, but we must assume that this is the pattern for the Early Church. In *Acts 6:1-6* we find that the people were instructed to select from among themselves certain men who qualified for this ministry. Very likely it would be men who were already serving and ministering to the people of God without a title. There is evidently a time for these to be proved *(I Timothy 3:10),* they are set before the local leaders and ministries, they are prayed over and set in by the leadership.

STUDY QUESTIONS FOR CHAPTER SEVEN

1. How does one demonstrate his submission to the Holy Spirit?

2. What are the five gifted ministries given by Christ to the Church?

3. How important are these ministries in the fulfillment of the ultimate plan of God?

4. Define each of these five ministries.

5. What is the distinction between the terms "elder," "bishop," and "pastor"?

6. What is the function of an elder?

7. What are eleven moral qualifications for an elder?

8. What are three domestic qualifications for an elder?

9. What are seven spiritual qualifications for an elder?

10. What is the only center of training mentioned in relation to the New Testament Church?

11. If the Church is not democratic, what is it?

12. What are ten qualifications for a deacon?

13. What are four qualifications for a deaconess?

CHAPTER EIGHT

The Church As The
Body of Christ

The Church
As The Body
Of Christ

Chapter Eight

We have already said in Chapter Six that one of the primary things that God is doing today involves a restoration of an awareness of and an appreciation for the Body of Christ. We said that God gave us the revelation of the Body of Christ that we might understand His purpose more fully, that we might understand His desire to use the present Body of Christ to minister life and healing in the same way that Christ ministered in His earthly walk. We have seen the proper relationship of the Head to this Body, and how Christ uses the ministries which He has set into the Body to direct, establish, perfect and lead the People of God. We have seen that a proper relationship to God's chain of command is necessary if we are to function as a normal healthy Body. When every member of the Body is rightly related to the whole, we can expect to see God's purpose being realized.

In past years we have seen man attempting to work out the purpose of God in his own way. We have seen those who have recognized a need to minister to the lives of people but lacked the knowledge of how this might be done. For years one man has tried to be the minister, when the Bible declares that we are to minister. For years we have seen the Body of Christ sit as spectators, watching a few minister. This could hardly be called a Body in ministry.

Some, however, have seen the tremendous spiritual weakness in such an approach and have reacted in an equally destructive manner. Having little or no knowledge of what God wanted to do in the Local Church, they have over reacted. So independent prayer meetings spring up that lack the system of checks provided by the New Testament structure and order. These groups seek to minister to one another, but they have no purpose, goals, outreach or oversight. They become a law unto themselves ignoring such scriptural principles as headship and submission to a local body. This reaction also fails to accomplish what God desires in relation to His Body. In most cases such groups end in confusion.

God's answer to all of these questions is in the Local Church. In the Local Church God has provided a way for the ministry of the Body to be accomplished. As we submit to God's chain of command, each member of the Body will be functioning and ministering in such a way as to bring the Plan of God to fulfillment.

In *Ephesians 4:11-12* we have a description of God's plan for perfecting the saints. God gave human oversight ministries with a view to perfecting the saints. If we take a look at this passage in the original Greek we get a tremendous insight into this plan. If one would translate this passage from the Greek using only the punctuation and the exact expressions found in the Greek it could be translated as follows, *"And He gave some apostles, and some prophets, and some evangelists, and some shepherds and teachers, with a view to the equipping of the saints for the work of ministry (service). . ."* (Translated from the Nestle-Aland Greek text). The New English Bible translates these verses as follows, *"And these were His gifts: some to be apostles, some prophets, some evangelists, some pastors and teachers, to equip God's people for work in His service. . ."*

What a tremendous thing to know that Christ did not give the five-fold ministry to do the work of ministry, but to bring the saints to a place of ministry. The ministry of the leadership is to help to bring the members of the Body of Christ into their perfect place of ministry or service. We will see in this chapter that God is using Christ's Body to accomplish His purposes, and every born-again believer has a place of function in this Body. Every true believer is to be a part of the total ministry of the Body.

50.   WHAT DOES THE BIBLE TEACH ABOUT THE BODY OF CHRIST?

Since the incarnation and the virgin birth of Jesus Christ, Christ has had a body. When Jesus Christ became man, He took on flesh and blood. He was made in the likeness of men *(Philippians 2:7)*. This body was a body prepared by the Spirit of God *(Luke 1:34-35, Hebrews 1:5)*. It was complete with all the intricacies of the human body. It was a many-membered body. In this body Jesus ministered on the earth. This body He used as He stretched forth His hands to heal. The physical body of Jesus was undefiled by sin. He could touch sinful men, and yet He was not defiled. In Him was no sin, which made His body absolutely incapable of sickness or death. In Him was life, and the life was the light of men *(John 1:4)*. He was full of life and the Spirit *(Luke 4:14)*.

This was the natural, physical body of Jesus Christ. This was the body through which Jesus ministered to the needs of men. This body, however, had its limitations. As long as Jesus walked on the earth He was limited by space and time. He could only be at a single place at any given time. This is why Jesus told his disciples that it was expedient that He should go away *(John 16:7)*. When Jesus ascended on high He gave the Spirit to direct the new SPIRITUAL Body of Christ, The Church. Christ now operates in and through this SPIRITUAL Body, He Himself being the Head. Since it is a spiritual Body, it must be spiritually discerned. The natural man or the natural eye can never fully comprehend the reality of such a Body, and yet the Scripture clearly defines such a Body *(I Corinthians 2:14)*. Let us look at what the Bible says about this Body:

a)   Christ is presently within His People. This doesn't take away from the fact that He will visibly return at the end of the age, but the Bible teaches that He must first appear in His People before He will come for His own *(Malachi 3:1; Colossians 3:4; Psalms 102:16).*

Colossians 1:27 - "To whom God would make known what is the riches of the glory of this mystery among the Gentiles; which is Christ in you, the hope of glory."

Romans 8:9-10 - "But ye are not in the flesh, but in the Spirit, if so be that the Spirit of God dwell in you. Now if any man have not the Spirit of Christ, he is none of His. And if Christ be in you, the body is dead because of sin; but the Spirit is life because of right-eousness."

This group of people indwelt by the Spirit of God comprise the Church which is His Body *(Ephesians 1:23).*

b)   The Local Church is the visible embodiment of Jesus Christ on earth. This body is therefore virtually united to and indwelt by Christ.

Ephesians 5:30-32- "For we are members of His Body, of His flesh, and of His bones. For this cause shall a man leave his father and mother, and shall be joined unto his wife, and they two shall be one flesh. This is a great mystery: but I speak concerning Christ and the Church."

c)   Christ so identifies Himself with the Church that it is impossible to separate Christ from His Church. Saul found out that, when you persecute the Church, you persecute Christ Himself *(Acts 9:1-6).*

Matthew 10:40 - "He that receiveth you receiveth Me, and he that receiveth Me receiveth Him that sent me."

Ephesians 5:29 - "For no man ever yet hated his own flesh, but nourisheth and cherisheth it, even as the Lord the Church."

d) The Local Church is made up of flesh and blood just as Jesus' earthly body was made up of flesh and blood *(I Corinthians 6:15-20; 11:29-32).*

Hebrews 2:14 - "Forasmuch then as the children are partakers of flesh and blood, He also Himself took part of the same; that through death He might destroy him that had the power over death, that is, the devil."

e) When a man is born again he is no longer his own, but He becomes part of the Body of Christ. Every believer is an important part of this spiritual Body *(I Corinthians 6:15-20).*

I Corinthians 6:15 - "Know ye not that your bodies are the members of Christ? Shall I then take the members of Christ, and make them the members of an harlot? God forbid."

New English - "Do you not know that your bodies are limbs and organs of Christ? Shall I then take from Christ His bodily parts and make them over to an harlot? God forbid."

I Corinthians 12:27 - "Now ye are the Body of Christ, and members in particular."

New English - "Now you are Christ's Body, and each of you a limb or organ of it."

f) Christ presently desires to live His life through His present spiritual Body, the Church.

Galatians 2:20 - "I am crucified with Christ: nevertheless I live; yet not I, but Christ liveth in me: and the life which I now live in the flesh I live by the faith of the Son of God, who loved me, and gave Himself for me."

New English - "I have been crucified with Christ: the life I now live is not my life, but the life which Christ lives in me; and my present bodily life is lived by faith in the Son of God, who loved me and sacrificed Himself for me."

g) Even as Christ only had one physical body, He only has one spiritual Body. The Lord tells us that there is one Body *(Ephesians 4:4)*. It does not say there will be one Body someday before the Lord comes, but there is one Body now. This Body is comprised of both Jew and Gentile – Everyone who has received Christ is accepted in the beloved *(Ephesians 2:16, Colossians 1:24-27)*.

Ephesians 2:16 - "And that He might reconcile both unto God in one body by the cross, having slain the enmity thereby."

h) Such a union of Christ and the Church is a great mystery. It was a plan and purpose hid in God from the foundation of the world and was only disclosed at the cross.

Ephesians 3:3-6 - "How that by revelation He made known unto me the mystery; (as I wrote afore in few words, whereby, when ye read, ye may understand my knowledge in the mystery of Christ) which in other ages was not made known unto the sons of men, as it is now revealed unto His holy apostles and prophets by the Spirit; that the Gentiles should be fellowheirs, and of the same Body, and partakers of His promise in Christ by the Gospel."

i) The Body of Christ is a growing Body. There is nothing outside of Christ and His Body that contributes anything to this Body. Jesus Christ provides all that is necessary to the Body for its *"edification ." (Ephesians 4:12)*.

j)   Each member of this Body of Christ is vitally joined to Christ and to every other believer *(Ephesians 4:16)*. There are many who would say that they only need Christ. Christ is presently ministering through this Body. To cut yourself off from this Body is to cut yourself off from Christ.

51.   WHY IS THE UNITY OF THE BODY SO IMPORTANT?

The Bible says there is but ONE Body *(Ephesians 4:4)*. It is not difficult to see that if a natural body is not flowing together, it will not function properly. The same is true in the spiritual realm. If we are to function effectively, we need to function harmoniously. This is what God desires to do in these days. His desire is to gather together the Body of Christ. We are not speaking of an external unity, although that is bound to follow, but we are talking about a real internal unity brought about by the Spirit of God.

Unity is a tremendous force. Even in the natural when men get together with a common interest, purpose and goal, they can accomplish the impossible. God recognized this when He confounded the tongues of man at Babel *(Genesis 11)*. If such a principle is true in the natural, how much more powerful is a spiritual Body of people banded together with a common interest, purpose and goal. Satan's desire is to keep the Body of Christ confounded. This is the only way that he can keep his dominion.

In the restoration in the days of Nehemiah, the secret to their success was not in lack of opposition. They had plenty of opposition. But the reason they were able to finish the work of restoration was simply because of this type of unity. Every man was in his place doing his own work. They didn't have three or four men trying to do the same job, leaving other positions desolate and unguarded, but they all recognized one another's ministry, and they all flowed together *(Nehemiah 4)*.

If we are going to have this kind of unity, we are going to have to recognize and receive the ministry of others. This is what the whole Body of Christ is all about. The following is a scriptural outline of what our relationship is to be to one another in the Body of Christ if we are going to minister effectively as a Body:

a)   In order to minister as a Body we must recognize that we are members one of another *(Romans 12:4-5; I Corinthians 6:15; 12:7-27; Ephesians 4:16, 25; 5:30)*.

      I Corinthians 10:17 - "For we being many are one bread, and one Body: for we are all partakers of that one bread."

b)   In order to minister as a Body the members of the Body must be at peace with each other *(Mark 9:50; Matthew 5:23; I Thessalonians 5:13)*.

      1.   A Body at peace does not hold grudges *(James 5:9; I Peter 4:9)*.
      2.   A Body at peace does not speak evil (gossip will kill Body ministry *(James 4:11)*.
      3.   A Body at peace does not esteem one member higher than another *(I Timothy 5:21; I Corinthians 12:25)*.
      4.   A Body at peace does not judge another harshly *(Romans 2:1; 14:13)*.

c)   In order to minister as a Body the members of the Body must seek the interest of the other members of the Body. They must not be self-centered.

      1.   In honor they prefer one another *(Romans 12:10; Philippians 2:3-4; I Peter 5:5)*.
      2.   They are not puffed up against another thinking that their own ministry is greater than that of others *(I Corinthians 4:6-7)*.
      3.   They bear one another's burdens *(Galatians 6:2)*.

4.   They are considerate of one another *(Hebrews 10:24-25; Ephesians 5:33)*.

5.   They submit to one another in true humility *(Ephesians 5:21)*.

6.   They serve one another in love *(John 13:34-35; I Thessalonians 3:12; 4:9)*.

d)   In order to minister as a Body the members of the Body will always seek to strengthen other members *(Ephesians 4:16; I Thessalonians 5:11; Romans 14:19)*.

When all these things are in order we are ready to minister to others as the Body of Chirst.

a)   We can exhort one another *(Hebrews 3:13; 10:25)*.

b)   We can admonish one another *(Romans 15:14; Colossians 3:16)*.

c)   We can have true compassion one to another *(I Peter 3:8)*.

d)   We can comfort one another *(I Thessalonians 4:18; II Corinthians 1:4)*.

e)   We can pray for one another *(James 5:16)*.

Romans 15:5-6 (Amplified Bible) - "Now may the God who gives the power of patient endurance and who supplies encouragement, grant you to live in such mutual harmony and such full sympathy with one another, in accord with Christ Jesus, that together you may (unanimously) with united hearts and one voice, praise and glorify the God and Father of our Lord Jesus Christ, the Messiah."

52.   HOW DOES THE BODY OF CHRIST FUNCTION?

Before reading any further we suggest that you read *I Corinthians 12 - 14*.

I Corinthians 12 - 14 gives us the answer as to how this

Body is to function. Paul begins *chapter 12* by saying, *"Now concerning spirituals, brethren, I would not have you ignorant"* (The original Greek does not have the word "gifts," it is supplied by the translators. A more appropriate translation would be "spiritual things"). This is how he introduces his discussion of the ministry of the Body. He goes on to emphasize the diversity of ministry in the Body of Christ. There are diversities of gifts; there are diversities of administrations (ministries or services); and there are diversities of operations (works or activities); but it is all the same Spirit. It is actually God who is working all of these things in all of the members of the Body of Christ. Paul wants us to see that we are fellow workers with God- - God working in us.

We have to see the picture that Paul is drawing for us. In Christ is the fulness of all ministry, gifts and operations. He is all in all. When He ascended on high His fulness was simply broken down and distributed by the Spirit to different members of the Body of Christ. We have all been made partakers of the ministry of Christ. Even as each member of the natural body has a function, so also every member of the Body of Christ has a function. Even as each member of the natural body is of benefit to the total body, so also every member of the Body of Christ has a vital place of service and function. Each member has gifts differing according to the grace given *(Romans 12:6),* but each member has a vital part.

Just because you are not the hand or one of the five-fold ministry does not mean you are not part of the Body. You may be a foot which is necessary for service in the ministry of a deacon (servant). Just because you are not the eye and do not have deep spiritual insight into the Word of God does not mean that you are not part of the Body. You may be an ear, one who has an intimate relationship to the Head so as to hear from God in a unique way, or you may be the smelling, one who is able to discern the mind of God. We have to see that all of these things are important to the functioning of the total Body. We cannot do without the eye, ear, foot, hand or smelling. They are all necessary to the proper functioning of the Body.

The Body functions best when each member of the Body is doing what God has intended for it to do. If the foot tries to be a hand it will never be successful. It will never eat as efficiently as the hand. It will never play a musical instrument as skillfully as the hand. It can only expect a life of frustration and failure. But if the foot seeks only to fulfill the ministry that God has given to it, it will find both fulfillment and accomplishment. If it is called to be a foot and is trying to be a hand, who is going to carry the body to its destination. The hand can't do it. It wasn't made to support the weight of the body. If the foot is trying to be the hand, there is some ministry that is being neglected. We have to see that God doesn't judge us on the basis of whether or not we were the hand or the foot. He judges us on the basis of how faithful we were with what He has given us to do, and that is different for each member of the Body.

Our biggest problem is that we compare or rate ministries. God never does. God does not hold one ministry above another. To Him they are all important. He gives ministries severally as He wills, and He knows it. All He desires is a usable vessel that will be faithful to do that which He was willed.

The Body functions best when every member of the Body is doing what God has called him to do. Every member of the Body needs to seek God about what they should be doing in terms of ministry. There is no member of the Body that does not have a function. If God has put you in the Body, you have a place of ministry.

I Corinthians 14:26 - "How is it then, brethren? When ye come together, every one of you hath a psalm, hath a doctrine, hath a tongue, hath a revelation, hath an interpretation. Let all things be done unto edifying."

Romans 12:6-8 - "Having then gifts differing according to the grace that is given to us, whether prophecy, let us prophesy according to the proportion of faith: Or ministry, let us wait on our ministering: or he that teacheth, on teaching; or he that exhorteth, on exhorta-

*tion: he that giveth, let him do it with simplicity; he
that ruleth, with diligence; he that showeth mercy, with
cheerfulness.''*

53. CAN A BELIEVER FIND FULFILLMENT APART FROM AN IDENTIFICATION WITH THE LOCAL CHURCH?

Because of the unique purpose which God has made
known, because of the tremendous plan God has for
the Body and because of the intricate interrelation-
ships in the Body, no true believer can find fulfillment
and accomplishment outside of the Body of Christ, the
Church. Just as Christ's natural body was visible, even so
His present Body has its visible expression. To fail to
identify with the visible Body of Christ or the Local
Church is to sever yourself from the Body. As soon as
you cut off your foot, that foot looses its function.
The foot only has a function as it relates to the body.
Our ministries are only useful or edifying to the Body as
they are properly related to the Body. When they are
properly related, the life giving blood will flow to
cleanse, heal and nourish each and every member of
the Body.

There is something even more severe if we cut ourselves
off from the Church, the Body of Christ. When a person rejects the Body, he rejects the Head. A severed foot no longer
responds to the commands and directions of the brain. When
a person rejects the Body, he rejects God's chain of command
and becomes a law unto himself. This is lawlessness. God calls
it rebellion.

There are many today who desire to be used of God,
but they refuse to come under the authority of the Body of
Christ. When we understand what the Body means to God, it
is not hard for us to see why rebellion is condemned so harshly
by Him *(Isaiah 1:19-23).*

I Samuel 15:23 - *"For rebellion is as the sin of witchcraft, and stubbornness is as iniquity and idolatry. Because thou hast rejected the Word of the Lord, he hath also rejected thee from being king."*

Proverbs 17:11 - *"An evil man seeketh only rebellion: therefore a cruel messenger shall be sent against him."*

Jeremiah 28:16 - *"Therefore thus saith the Lord; Behold, I will cast thee from off the face of the earth: this year thou shalt die, because thou has taught rebellion against the Lord."*

Psalms 68:6 - *"God setteth the solitary in families: he bringeth out those which are bound with chains: but the rebellious dwell in a dry land."*

Matthew 7:21-23 - *"Not every one that saith unto me, Lord, Lord, shall enter into the kingdom of heaven; but he that doeth the will of my Father which is in heaven. Many will say to me in that day, Lord, Lord, have we not prophesied in thy name? and in thy name have cast out devils? and in thy name done many wonderful works? And then will I profess unto them, I never knew you: depart from me, ye that work iniquity.*

God gives us strict instructions not to forsake the assembling of ourselves together. As we gather as the Body of Christ, we will be strengthened, the Body will be built up and the purpose of God will be accomplished in and through Christ's Body, the Church.

Hebrews 10:25 - *"Not forsaking the assembling of ourselves together, as the manner of some is; but exhorting one another: and so much the more, as ye see the day approaching."*

STUDY QUESTIONS FOR CHAPTER EIGHT

1. What is the ministry of the five-fold ministry in relation to the Body of Christ?

2. Why was it expedient for Christ to physically leave the earth?

3. How does Christ presently carry on His ministry?

4. What is the visible expression of Christ on earth?

5. Why is unity important in days of restoration?

6. How does the Body of Christ function best?

7. Why is it so important to identify with a Local Church?

CHAPTER NINE

The Church As The Temple Of The Living God

The Church
As The Temple
Of The Living God

Chapter Nine

We have seen how God has given us various pictures of the Church throughout the Scripture that we might more fully comprehend the tremendous purpose which God has in His people. He gave us the picture of the Body of Christ that we might understand His purpose to use the present Body of Christ to minister in the same way that Christ ministered while on earth. Because the Church is so unique and there are so many facets to it, God has given us other pictures that further unfold His plan in the Church. We looked at a few of these in chapter six, and, while we don't have the space to discuss all of these comparisons, it is expedient that we look at one more of these pictures that has been given to us by God.

God refers to the Church as the Temple of God *(Ephesians 2:19-22; I Corinthians 3:16-17)*. In the Old Testament times God dwelt in a material temple, but the New Testament introduces us to His Spiritual Temple. The temple of the Old Testament is simply a shadow of the Spiritual Temple of God in the New Testament. Jesus Himself gives us the key to this interpretation in His discussion with the Jews in regard to the rebuilt temple of Herod. He said, *"Destroy this temple, and in three days I will raise it up . . . but He spake of the temple of His body" (John 2:19, 21)*. Here Jesus plainly compares His own body to a temple. Now we are the Body of Christ, and, hence, the Temple of God.

Jesus is the builder of this Temple *(Matthew 16:18)*, but He uses the ministries that He has placed in the Body to do much of the work. Christ Himself is the Chief Cornerstone

(Ephesians 2:20), the foundation is laid by the apostles and prophets *(Ephesians 2:20; Hebrews 6:1-2)*, but we all have a part through our ministry of love in adding to the edification or building up of the Temple *(Ephesians 4:16)*. Each member of the Body of Christ is also a living stone that is to find his place in the Temple structure *(I Peter 2:5)*. These stones are being cut and shaped and built upon the foundation which has been laid *(I Kings 5:17-18; 6:7)*. These stones are being fitly framed together *(Ephesians 2:21-22)*. God's purpose in giving us such a revelation of the Temple of God is that we might more fully comprehend His intention to bring the People of God together that He might fill us with the fulness of Himself *(Ephesians 3:19-21; 2:22)*.

There is much more involved in the Church, however, if it is to measure up to the privilege of being the Temple of God. The building of the Temple itself is great, for it is a building like no other building. It is a building with living stones that grow! The fact that God wants to fill this Temple with His fulness is exciting for in His presence is fulness of joy. But in every other temple in Scripture there was more involved than just a building and the presence of God although these are indispensible. Every other temple in the Old Testament had a PRIESTHOOD and SACRIFICES.

> *I Peter 2:5 - "Ye also, as lively stones, are built up a spiritual house, an holy priesthood, to offer up spiritual sacrifices, acceptable to God by Jesus Christ."*

54.   WHAT IS THE PRIESTHOOD IN THE NEW TESTAMENT TEMPLE OF GOD?

In the Old Testament God gave a priesthood under the law to the Children of Israel. God has always desired to have a righteous nation in priestly fellowship with Himself. This was His purpose in calling Isarel, that they might be a nation of priests. In fact, He offered to Israel exactly what He was later to give to the Church.

Exodus 19:5-6 - "Now therefore, if ye will obey My voice indeed, and keep My covenant, then ye shall be a peculiar treasure unto Me above all people: for all the earth is Mine: and ye shall be unto Me a kingdom of priests, and an holy nation."

Because of the disobedience of the Children of Israel, however, God did not make Israel a kingdom of priests. They did not fulfill the conditions of this promise. Instead God gave them an inferior priesthood as a tutor and a governor to bring them to Christ in whom they could once again become heirs to this same promise. God gave to Israel the Aaronic priesthood. Far from the whole nation being a kingdom of priests, God singled out the tribe of Levi to act as priests and handle the holy things. This Aaronic priesthood was not God's ideal. In fact, it was a substitute for the ideal. It actually became a shadow of the priesthood that God desired to give.

The priesthood of which God desires us to become partakers is described for us in *Hebrews 5 - 7*. This priesthood has a High Priest, the Lord Jesus Christ *(Hebrews 2:17; 4:14; 6:20)*. Just the fact that there is a High Priest implies that there are other priests in the priesthood, or the designation HIGH Priest would be superfluous. This priesthood is the Melchizedek Priesthood. This is the priesthood that was offered to Israel, God's chosen people *(Exodus 19:5-7)*. Because they failed to enter into this priesthood, it was taken from them and given to another, the Lord Jesus Christ *(Psalms 110:1-2)*. What they forfeited on the basis of disobedience, Jesus inherited on the basis of His perfect obedience *(Hebrews 5:8-9)*. As we stand in Him, therefore, we can become partakers of this everlasting priesthood.

It is not our purpose at this time to give a detailed analysis of this priesthood, for it is a lengthy study. Yet, it is beneficial at this point to look at a few key verses in regard to this priesthood and its implications.

Hebrews 7:11-17 - "If therefore perfection were by the Levitical priesthood, (for under it the people received

*the law) what further need was there that another
priest should rise after the order of Melchisedec, and not
be called after the order of Aaron? For the priesthood
being changed, there is made of necessity a change also
of the law. For He of whom these things are spoken
pertaineth to another tribe, of which no man gave attendance at the altar. For it is evident that our Lord
sprang out of Juda; of which tribe Moses spake nothing
concerning priesthood. And it is far more evident: for
that after the similitude of Melchisedec there ariseth
another priest, who is made, not after the law of a
carnal commandment, but after the power of an endless
life. For he testifieth, Thou art a priest forever after
the order of Melchisedec."*

*Hebrews 5:1 - "For every high priest taken from among
men is ordained for men in things pertaining to God,
that he may offer both gifts and sacrifices for sins."*

55. WHAT ARE THE SACRIFICES OFFERED BY THE NEW TESTAMENT PRIESTS?

In *Hebrews 5:1* we just learned that a priest is ordained
to offer gifts and sacrifices *(Hebrews 8:3)*. Christ as
our High Priest has offered such gifts and sacrifices.
But we, as kings and priests unto God also have sacrifices to offer. Priestly fellowship is always grounded on
the basis of sacrifice. This principle holds true in both
the Old and New Testaments. When the patriarchs
desired to meet with God, they always sacrificed. They
built an altar unto God, knowing that if they were to
have His presence, they must sacrifice. Jacob built an
altar; Abraham built an altar; Elijah built an altar on
Carmel. In all of these many cases, God never failed to
meet with these individuals who approached on the
basis of sacrifice. God never denies or changes His
principles. We too must prepare an altar of sacrifice to
meet with God – not a literal altar to sacrifice a literal

animal, but we are priests born to offer "spiritual sac-rifices" unto the Lord. In Christ we become partakers of that ROYAL PRIESTHOOD *"to offer up spiritual sacrifices, acceptable to God by Jesus Christ" (I Peter 2:5).*

There are many sacrifices that the New Testament priest is ordained to offer. These include the following:

a)   YOURSELVES - The New Testament teaches that we are to yield ourselves to God *(Romans 6:13).* God wants to use all of our members as instruments of His glory. Each day we need to yield our members afresh to this tremendously high calling. In the Old Testament we have a picture of this in Solomon who had a scaffold built that was the exact size of the Brazen Altar on which all of the Tabernacle sacrifices were offered. He placed this scaffold in the midst of the court, stood upon it, *"Kneeled down before all the congregation of Israel, and spread his hands toward heaven" (II Chron-icles 6:13).* Solomon was actually presenting himself a living sacrifice. God desires for us to present ourselves upon the altar as a living sacrifice.

Romans 12:1-2 - "I beseech you therefore, breth-ren, by the mercies of God, that ye present your bodies a living sacrifice, holy, acceptable unto God, which is your reasonable service. And be not conformed to this world: but be ye transformed by the renewing of your mind, that ye may prove what is that good, and acceptable, and perfect, will of God."

Part of this sacrifice involves cutting ourselves off from the world system. How do we present ourselves holy and acceptable unto God? By not being conformed to this world system. This means we will have to sacrifice and give up our worldly desires and let God transplant His perfect desires in us giving us the desires of our heart *(Psalms 37:4).*

This sacrifice needs to be a daily offering of ourselves afresh. As we offer ourselves, spirit, soul and body, God promises to use us for His glory.

b)   YOUR TIME - Paul tells us of the importance of redeeming the time *(Ephesians 5:16; Colossians 4:5)*. God has given us time that we might give it back to Him. He has given it to us as a trust and a stewardship and, therefore, holds us accountable for our use of it. This sacrifice grows more and more essential as the days of His coming draw near. Every hour that passes brings us that much closer to that day when time shall be no more. God desires that we sacrifice our time for His use.

c)   YOUR SUBSTANCE - Everything that we own belongs to God. What do we have that was not given to us? In the Old Testament the Children of Israel were obligated to give tithes unto God. In the New Testament we are called to a higher law; we are obliged to put all that we have at His disposal. God promises to take care of our needs so we can communicate as He desires. The Philippian Christians were willing to offer such sacrifices to God which, Paul says, were pleasing to God *(Philippians 4:18)*. He says that such a sacrifice was an odor of sweet savor. The sweet savor offerings of the Old Testament were those offerings that were given not from compulsion, but voluntarily of the giver's own free will. God desires us to give of our substance in like manner. He desires us to give of our own free will without a specific command. This sacrifice pleases God.

This sacrifice involves two different aspects. There is the giving of our substance to the storehouse, and there is the communicating of our substance to those of our brethren who are in need. Even in the Old Testament God gave instruction for how the Israelites were to care for the needy in their midst *(Deuteronomy 15:7-18)*, and He gives strict warning to those who build up their own barns and neglect the needs of those around them *(Deuteronomy 8:11-18; Luke 12:15-31)*. God is interested in our money. How we spend our money is a good indication of where our heart is *(Matthew 6:21)*. If you want to know how you are doing in regard to this spiritual sacrifice, read your check stubs.

Hebrews 13:16 - "Do not forget or neglect to do kindness and good, to be generous and distribute and contribute to the needs (of the Church as embodiment and proof of fellowship), for such sacrifices are well-pleasing to God."

d)   YOUR GOOD WORKS - Faith without works is dead *(James 2:20)*. God wants us to do good *(Hebrews 13:16)*. He has called us to a life of faith, but a life of faith will produce the fruit of faith — obedience. A vital, living faith will always bring forth good works. These do not gain slavation for you, but they are something that we can offer to God on the basis of what He has done for us. Our righteousness is to exceed that of the scribes and pharisees *(Matthew 5:20)*, because we have been empowered by God in a way that the scribes and pharisees were not. You will know the People of God by their fruit *(Matthew 7:16)*.

Hebrews 13:16 - "But to do good and to communicate forget not: for with such sacrifices God is well pleased."

e)   YOUR FRUIT - God desires for us to declare His glory to the ends of the earth. As we give ourselves, our time, our substance and our works to Him, there is bound to be fruit from the earth *(Isaiah 66:19-20)*. We have the privilege as priests unto God to offer these back to God as an offering acceptable unto Him.

Romans 15:16 - " That I should be the minister of Jesus Christ to the Gentiles, ministering the gospel of God, that the offering up of the Gentiles might be acceptable, being sanctified by the Holy Ghost."

f)   SACRIFICE OF JOY - There is a difference between the joy of the Lord and a naturally joyful and exuberant spirit. Some people are naturally happy and outgoing. This type of joy involves no real sacrifice. There are times, however, when we are not of this disposition. There are times when it is very difficult to enter into the aspect of praise that involves the expression of joy. At these times joy becomes a sacrifice. As a priest unto God we have the privilege of offering this sacrifice of joy to God. As we learn to place our confidence in the Word and promises of God we will come to a place where we will be able to rejoice even in times of distress *(II Corinthians 4:8-10).* Naturally speaking there may be nothing to cause one to rejoice, but we will still lift our voice in joyous shouts of praise. A more literal rendering of this sacrifice as it is used in the Hebrew would be a "sacrifice of shouting." This would seem to imply that this sacrifice involves more than just an inner expression of joy, but it involves a life of Christian victory.

Psalms 27:6 - "And now shall mine head be lifted up above mine enemies round about me: therefore will I offer in His tabernacle sacrifices of joy; I will sing, yea, I will sing praises unto the Lord."

Because of the testimony that the People of God carry in these last days, the time is coming when men will revile us and speak evil of us. They will persecute the truth in their ignorance. In that day, we are not to be sad or worry, but we are to *"leap for joy" (Luke 6: 22-23).* For us to do this will involve our ability to offer the sacrifice of joy unto God. This sacrifice of joy which can only spring from a heart of faith will actually produce joy. This joy will be the strength of the People of God *(Nehemiah 8:10)* and a tremendous testimony to the uttermost parts of the earth.

g) SACRIFICE OF THANKSGIVING - Even under the law age God instituted the sacrifice of thanksgiving *(Leviticus 7:12)*. It is so easy to be thankful when we feel we have something for which we should be thankful. But to give God the sacrifice of thanksgiving is to give thanks for everything. It is this sacrifice that will cause us to lift up our hands and our voices and thank God in even the most adverse of circumstances realizing that God is in control of all the affairs of our life and that all of His dealings with us are to lead us into green pastures and beside still waters. Many times this will involve much sacrifice on our part, but this sacrifice is pleasing to God.

Jonah was in the most terrible of circumstances *(Jonah 2:9)*. He was in the belly of a fish where the natural eye could see nothing for which to be thankful, no cause for thanksgiving. But even here, something of God in Jonah was greater than Jonah's natural flesh and circumstances, and Jonah refused to let his spirit be bound. In *Chapter 2* of Jonah's account we find Jonah trying everything to no avail. He repented, he cried unto God, he confessed that he was not *"observing lying vanities,"* but in *verse 9*, when he sacrificed to God with a voice of thanksgiving, immediately the fish became ill. A thankful prophet was too much for the fish.

The secret to the sacrifice of thanksgiving involves the hearing ear and the believing heart. *"Faith cometh by hearing"* *(Romans 10:17)*. When we sacrifice with the voice of thanksgiving, our ears hear what our mouth declares. This confession produces faith in the heart. It is this faith which causes our deliverance. It is the faith of a people who have learned to give thanks in every situation that will cause the world to believe.

Psalms 107:22 - "And let them sacrifice the sacrifices of thanksgiving, and declare His works with rejoicing."

Psalms 116:17 - "I will offer to thee the sacrifices of thanksgiving, and call upon the name of the Lord."

h) SACRIFICE OF PRAISE - A blessing is something which you receive when you come into the House of God, but the "sacrifice" of praise is something that you bring with you. It is something that we offer to the Lord not on the basis of our circumstances or our feelings, but on the basis of our revelation of God and His greatness, and our desire to please Him and obey His Word *(Jeremiah 17:26)*.

Hebrews 13:15, 16b - "By Him therefore let us offer the sacrifice of praise to God continually, that is, the fruit of our lips giving thanks to his name. . .for with such sacrifices God is well pleased."

Jeremiah 33:11 - "The voice of joy, and the voice of gladness, the voice of the bridegroom and the voice of the bride, the voice of them that shall say, Praise the Lord of hosts: for the Lord is good; for His mercy endureth forever: and of them that shall bring the sacrifice of praise into the House of the Lord."

As A Royal Priesthood we have the privilege of being both priest and offering even as Christ offered Himself. As kings and priests unto God part of our ministry involves service at the Altar of Incense *(Revelation 5:10; 8:3-4)*. Prayer and praise are the spiritual sacrifices that are offered at the Altar of Incense. It is here that God comes down and meets with His people *(Exodus 29:42)*.

The apostle Paul understood this principle of praise.

Paul had his hands and feet in stocks, yet he would not allow his spirit to be bound *(Acts 16:25)*. In the midst of adverse circumstances he offered to God the sacrifice of praise. It was in this atmosphere of praise that God brought deliverance.

The Scripture indicates that God, who is holy, inhabits or lives in the praises of His people. If we desire God to come down and dwell in the midst of His people, it is our responsibility to offer the sacrifice of praise continually which will create the atmosphere in which God chooses to dwell. People often wonder if perhaps God has forsaken them in a particular situation, but often times their attitude is far from one of praise. As we begin to enter into this sacrifice of praise in every situation, we will begin to experience something of the abiding presence of God.

i)   A BROKEN AND A CONTRITE HEART - God is never as interested in external sacrifices as He is in a heart that is rightly related to Him. If the heart relationship is right, none of the other sacrifices will be a problem. But if the heart relationship is not right, all the other sacrifices will be mere forms. It is at this point that our righteousness exceeds that of the scribes and pharisees. It is from this heart condition that WORSHIP springs forth. True worship can only ascend from a heart that has been broken before God. It can only come from the lips of one who realizes his own unworthiness and, at the same time, beholds the magnificence of God. God desires people to worship Him in spirit and in truth *(John 4:24)*. A broken and a contrite heart can produce nothing else.

Psalms 51:17- "The sacrifices of God are a broken spirit: a broken and a contrite heart, O God, Thou wilt not despise."

We have seen at least nine spiritual sacrifices that we are to offer to God. The first five have to do with the area of the physical and material realms. God wants us to sacrifice our possessions and offer them for His unconditional use. The next three deal with the area of the mind, will and emotions. They are attitudes that God wants us to offer to Him. God wants all of our affections to be centered in Him. The last sacrifice has to do with the center of all sacrifice, the spirit realm. God wants to possess us spirit, soul and body.

SPIRITUAL SACRIFICES

God responds to a people who give freely unto the Lord. As we present ourselves to Him, He abundantly blesses us. As we freely give, the Lord freely gives. As we mete out, so it shall be meted unto us *(Matthew 7:2)*. King David knew this principle in God, and he also realized the abundance of God's provision. Today God is looking for "cheerful givers" not only in finances, but also in every other spiritual sacrifice. He is looking for a people who are willing to be gathered together having made a covenant by sacrifice. He is looking for a people who will accept the cost of discipleship.

Psalms 50:5 - "Gather My saints together unto Me; those that have made a covenant with Me by sacrifice."

Psalms 54:6 - "I will freely sacrifice unto Thee: I will praise Thy name, O Lord; for it is good."

II Samuel 24:24 - ". . .neither will I offer burnt offerings unto the Lord my God of that which cost me nothing."

These sacrifices that have been outlined for us by God are essential to spiritual growth. In fact, the writer of the Hebrews indicates that these are better sacrifices than those offered under the old covenant *(9:23)*, and they are instrumental in bringing us to perfection *(10:1)*. In order for the Church to be the Temple of God, it is going to have to be built on the basis of sacrifices. As kings and priests unto God we have the privilege of ministering unto God in this way.

STUDY QUESTIONS FOR CHAPTER NINE

1. What two elements must the Church contain if it is to be the Temple of God?

2. What is the priesthood in the New Testament Temple of God?

3. List nine spiritual sacrifices that are part of New Testament worship.

4. How do we present ourselves a living sacrifice unto God?

5. What two aspects are involved in the giving of our substance to God?

6. What three sacrifices involve our control over the soul-life?

7. What sacrifice is foundational to all the other sacrifices?

CHAPTER TEN

The Church As The
Tabernacle Of David

The Church
As The Tabernacle
Of David

Chapter Ten

In the previous chapter we dealt with the Church as the Temple of God. We laid particular emphasis on the spiritual sacrifices connected with that Temple. You may wonder why such an emphasis in a book on restoration. Hasn't the Church always been a place of sacrifice? Yes, it has, but God in these latter days seems to be emphasizing this aspect of Church life. He is particularly laying stress on the areas of praise and worship. In the Dark Ages we saw how the absence of a vital experience of the Spirit led men to write down liturgies that would prescribe a form of worship. Many of these liturgies were Word based and appear to be quite sound doctrinally, but the biggest problem is that they do not allow for the Spirit to move in and through a body of people who are rightly related to Him. They leave no room for individual expression of heartfelt praise and worship unto God. Repetition of a mere form can never bring life. It may have been life the first time it was done, but to continue in any form will not maintain that life which initiated it.

The area of Scripture that God has quickened to the Church in these last days has to do with the restoration of the Tabernacle of David. The Tabernacle of David is a very little known subject. Most people have never even heard of the Tabernacle of David. The reason may be that God has in a measure reserved the understanding of this Tabernacle for the Church of the last days. He has reserved it for the Church that will be instrumental in dealing with Satan and his kingdom.

Amos 9:11 - "In that day will I raise up the tabernacle of David that is fallen, and close up the breaches thereof; and I will raise up his ruins, and I will build it as in the days of old."

As the New Testament Church was being established there arose considerable problems in relation to many of the Jews who accepted Christ. They taught that to accept Christ you also had to keep the whole law of Moses. These Jews didn't see that the law was a schoolmaster to bring them to Christ. This question got so heated that many of the early Church leaders got together to discuss what should be done. They met in Jerusalem and discussed the matter openly. *Acts 15* is the record of this meeting. We find that Peter had something to say, Paul and Barnabas gave a report, but James under the inspiration of the Holy Spirit settled the issue by opening up the prophecy found in *Amos* that God would bring in the Gentiles and raise up the Tabernacle of David. He applies the Tabernacle of David to the Church, the melting pot for both Jew and Gentile, bond and free. Thus, the Church of the New Testament is the rebuilt Tabernacle of David.

Acts 15:15-17 - "And to this agree the words of the prophets; as it is written, After this I will return, and will build again the tabernacle of David, which is fallen down; and I will build again the ruins thereof, and I will set it up: that the residue of men might seek after the Lord, and all the Gentiles, upon whom My name is called, saith the Lord, who doeth all these things."

In order for us to fully comprehend how James could make such a statement, it is necessary for us to have a basic understanding of Israel's order of worship throughout their long history. Throughout the Old Testament God gave a progressive revelation of how man could approach unto the living God. Since the fall of man, man has not been in free fellowship with the Father. God, however, has always desired to fellowship with His creation. Therefore He has provided a way whereby we might fellowship with Him. To the patriarchs God revealed the altar and the blood sacrifice through which man could approach unto God. The only way man could come to God was through sacrifice. He had to come on the basis of a slain animal. He had to come on the basis of the death of another – a sinless substitute.

Later through Moses God revealed the Tabernacle of Moses that He might commune with His chosen NATION and that He might dwell among them *(Exodus 25:8)*. This Tabernacle was also founded upon animal sacrifices. Those who approached had to come on the basis of sinless blood. In this Tabernacle there were three compartments, the Outer Court, the Holy Place and the Holy of Holies or Most Holy Place. Any circumcised person could enter into the Outer Court providing he came on the basis of the blood. The Outer Court enclosed the Brazen Altar for sacrifice and the Brazen Laver which was used for cleansing. Within this Outer Court was a covered sanctuary which was divided by a veil into the Holy Place and the Most Holy Place. Only the priests were allowed to minister before the Golden Candlestick, the Golden Table of Shewbread, and the Golden Altar of Incense. The Holy

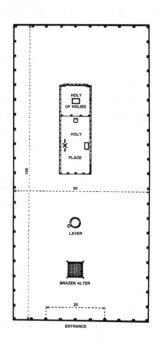

Place was separated from the Most Holy Place by the veil. Beyond this veil, in the Most Holy Place was the Ark of the Covenant. It was upon this piece of furniture that God chose to dwell in visible manifestation *(Exodus 40:33-38; Psalms 80:1)*. It was from off of this piece of furniture that God chose to speak to His people *(Leviticus 1:1)*. This was the only piece of furniture in the Most Holy Place. The Most Holy Place was off limits to everyone but the High Priest. And he could only enter in once a year with the blood of a bullock on the great Day of Atonement.

The Tabernacle of Moses was the way of approach that God provided for Israel. To them it was absolutely real in every respect. We look back to it as a type of what God was to do in Christ. Since Christ THE LAMB has been slain, God is no longer interested in animal sacrifices and animal blood. He is no longer interested in this form of worship, for the way has been opened. He now desires worship in spirit and in truth. Inspite of this, however, the Tabernacle of Moses offers a type study of God's work in Christ and the Church. We might summarize some of the significance of the Tabernacle of Moses as follows:

TABERNACLE STRUCTURE	THE LORD JESUS CHRIST	OUR PERSONAL EXPERIENCE
1. Brazen Altar	Our Perfect Sacrifice	Repentance and Acceptance
2. Brazen Laver	Our Sanctifier, Cleanser	Water Baptism
3. Golden Candlestick	Our Light	Apostles Doctrine
4. Table of Shewbread	Our Bread of Life	Breaking of Bread
5. Altar of Incense	Our Intercessor	Prayers
6. Ark of the Covenant	Our Life	Fellowship *(Acts 2:38-42)*

(Note: For a more detailed study of this subject see: The Tabernacle of Moses by Kevin J. Conner).

Between the Tabernacle of Moses and the Temple of Solomon God ordained the Tabernacle of David. This structure only remained for approximately 40 years. It is very much different from any other structure in the Old Testament. Because of James' interpretation of this structure in the New Testament, we can assume that it was a 40 year glimpse of what God was to do in the Church. For this reason we want to briefly look at what was involved in this Tabernacle (note: This is far from a complete study of the Tabernacle of David. A complete study would be a work in itself. Therefore we will limit ourselves to a few basic characterisitics of this Tabernacle).

The Tabernacle of David was given by revelation to King David when he desired to bring the Ark back after it had been captured by the Philistines many years before. Saul never seemed to care much for the Ark, but David recognized the tremendous power of this piece of furniture. He recognized the importance of having this piece of furniture on which God had communicated with His people in times past. David knew that when the Ark was gone the glory had departed from Israel *(I Samuel 4:21-22)*. David knew that the presence of God was essential to any visitation, and he longed for the presence of God. When David finally was able to bring the Ark back, he didn't return it to the Tabernacle of Moses which was set up on Mt. Gibeon. Instead, he brought it to Mt. Zion in the city of David. He didn't set up another Tabernacle like the one which was set up on Mt. Gibeon with the three compartments and the various pieces of furniture. David set up a single tent to house a single piece of furniture, the ARK OF THE COVENANT (See: *I Chronicles 13 - 16; II Samuel 6:17-19)*.

This meant that at this point we have two Tabernacles set up. The Tabernacle of Moses is set up on Mt. Gibeon without the presence of the Lord *(I Chronicles 16:37-43; 21: 28-30)*, while the Tabernacle of David was set up on Mt. Zion with the presence of the Lord *(II Samuel 6:17; II Chronicles 5:2)*. There was actually a transplanting of the Most Holy Place to Mt. Zion. During this time there were two companies of priests. Those at Gibeon functioned as always, going through all the forms and rituals that they had done for years without the presence of the Lord. Externally it looked exactly the same as always, but the glory had departed *(I Samuel 4:21)*. The second company of priests, however, moved in new areas of ministry. All of the priests had their chance to minister before the Ark because there was NO VEIL in the Tabernacle of David. Their ministry did not involve animal sacrifice, but they offered up spiritual sacrifices.

The Tabernacle of David is a picture of the Church. There was only one blood sacrifice in connection with the Tabernacle of David. When this Tabernacle was dedicated they offered up animal sacrifices, but from then on there were only spiritual sacrifices. The Church, also, is founded on the once-for-all blood sacrifice of THE LAMB of God. From the birth of the Church on we offer spiritual sacrifices acceptable unto God by Christ Jesus. In the Church all believers are priests unto God who are able to enter into God's presence and offer that which is pleasing unto God. We are able to enter into the presence of God because Jesus opened the way and the veil was rent.

The order of worship in the Tabernacle of David is of particular significance in light of what God is doing in these days to establish and rebuild the Tabernacle of David. Notice the following verses which speak of that order of worship in the Tabernacle of Daivd:

> *I Chronicles 15:28 - "Thus all Israel brought up the Ark of the Covenant of the Lord with shouting, and with sound of the cornet, and with trumpets, and with cymbals, making a noise with psalteries and harps."*

> *I Chronicles 16:4 - "And he (David) appointed certain of the Levites to minister before the Ark of the Lord, and to record, and to thank and praise the Lord God of Israel."*

> *I Chronicles 23:5 - "Moreover four thousand were porters; and four thousand praised the Lord with the instruments which I made, said David, to praise therewith."*

> *I Chronicles 25:5-6 - "All these were the sons of Heman the King's seer in the words of God, to lift up the horn.*

> *And God gave to Heman fourteen sons and three daughters. All these were under the hands of their father for song in the house of the Lord, with cymbals, psalteries, and harps, for the service of the house of God, according to the king's order to Asaph, Jeduthun, and Heman."*

The order of worship in the Tabernacle of David as opposed to that found in the Tabernacle of Moses has been summarized on the following page. The *Psalms,* for the most part, were birthed in the Tabernacle of David, and they are descriptive of the worship present there. In the New Testament there is no specific "order of worship" given for the Church, but Christ taught that He would fulfill in His Church all that was written in the Law, the Prophets and the Psalms concerning Him *(Luke 24:44).* God did not promise to restore the Tabernacle of Moses, His promise is to restore the Tabernacle of David. He tells us that we are not come unto Mt. Sinai (i.e. The Tabernacle of Moses), but we are come unto Mt. Zion (i.e. The Tabernacle of David – the Church), which is the Church of the firstborn *(Hebrews 12:18-23).* It is in the Tabernacle of David that we can find the order of worship for the New Testament Church. We have abundant evidence that the New Testament Church used the *Psalms* in worship more than anything else.

> *Ephesians 5:19 - "Speaking to yourselves in palms, and hymns and spiritual songs, singing and making melody in your heart to the Lord."*

> *Colossians 3:16 - "Let the Word of Christ dwell in you richly in all wisdom; teaching and admonishing one another in psalms and hymns and spiritual songs, singing with grace in your hearts to the Lord."*

With this in mind, it is not difficult for us to see that Mt. Zion and the worship on Mt. Zion is a very important study throughout the Scripture. Whenever Zion occurs it is relating truth that is of particular significance to the Church of

MT. SINAI

TABERNACLE OF MOSES

1. NO Singing
2. NO Music
3. NO Recording
4. NO Thanksgiving
5. NO Praise
6. NO Clapping
7. NO Shouting
8. NO Dancing
9. NO Lifting of Hands (except waving)
10. Joy was Commanded
11. Worship was afar off
12. Only High Priest ministered before Ark
13. Few Psalms (*Psalm 90 only*)
14. Said Amen to curses (*Deut. 27*)

MT. ZION

TABERNACLE OF DAVID

1. Singers with Singing (*I Chron. 15:16*)
2. Instruments and Music (*I Chron. 23:5*)
3. Recording (*I Chron. 16:4; Ps. 60:1*)
4. Sacrifice of Thanksgiving (*I Chron. 16:4,8,41*)
5. Sacrifice of Praise (*I Chron. 16:4,36*)
6. Clap Offerings (*Psalm 47:1*)
7. Shouts of Praise (*I Chron. 15:28*)
8. Dancing before the Lord (*I Chron. 16:29*)
9. Lifting of Hands (*Psalm 134*)
10. Heartfelt Rejoicing and Joy (*I Chron. 16:10, 27*)
11. The Way is Open
12. All Levites ministered before Ark
13. Much Psalm Singing (*I Chron. 16:7*)
14. Said Amen in Blessing (*I Chron. 16:36; Ps. 106:48*)

"For ye are not come unto Mt. Sinai. . .BUT YE ARE COME UNTO MT. ZION" Hebrews 12:22

the New Testament (See: *Psalms 2:6; 9:11-14; 48:1-12; 132:13-18; Isaiah 4:3-5; 12:6; 33:14-24; Joel 2:1; Micah 4: 2-4; Isaiah 16:1-5; 28:16; I Peter 2:6; Romans 9:33; Hebrews 12:22-24).*

With this background in mind we want to examine the order of worship in the *Psalms,* recognizing that this is our order of worship as well.

56.   **WHY SHOULD THE CHURCH BE A PLACE OF PRAISE AND WORSHIP?**

Whenever and wherever you find the People of God released from captivity (days of Restoration) there also comes a new release and desire to worship.

Psalms 126:1-3 - "When the Lord turned again the captivity of Zion, we were like them that dream. Then was our mouth filled with laughter, and our tongue with singing: then said they among the heathen, the Lord hath done great things for them. The Lord hath done great things for us; whereof we are glad."

It only takes a few minutes in a congregation to tell if they are experiencing a fresh visitation of the Presence of the Lord. A free people will worship freely. A captive people have no song nor desire to worship.

Psalms 137:1-4 - "By the rivers of Babylon, there we sat down, yea, we wept, when we remembered Zion. We hanged our harps upon the willows in the midst thereof. For there they that carried us away captive required of us a song; and they that wasted us required of us mirth, saying, Sing us one of the songs of Zion. How shall we sing the Lord's song in a strange land?"

The Key to understanding the Tabernacle of David is what happened there in terms of praise and worship. Before we discuss the way in which they worshipped in the Tabernacle of David, it is important for us to establish some reasons why we worship and praise the Lord (Note: At this time we will discuss praise and worship together, we will make a distinction between the two later). Praise and worship is one of the most important subjects in the Bible. There are more references to this subject than any other single subject. If the Word of God places such an emphasis on worship, we ought to do the same. There are at least fifteen reasons why the People of God will worship and bow down before the Lord their Maker. Five reasons are seen from God's point of view and ten reasons are from man's point of view.

a)   Praise and worship are important as sacrifices unto God *(Hebrews 13:15)*.

1)   God commands us to praise Him *(I Peter 2:9; Philippians 2:9-11; Psalms 67:3; 9:11)*. If we never had another word in the scripture regarding praise, this would be sufficient reason to praise God.

Psalms 22:23 - "Ye that fear the Lord, praise Him, all ye seed of Jacob, glorify Him; and fear Him, all ye seed of Israel."

I Chronicles 16:29 - "Give unto the Lord the glory due unto His name: bring an offering, and come before Him: worship the Lord in the beauty of holiness."

2)   God is worthy to be praised. God has shown abundant mercy and lovingkindness to his people *(Psalms 63:3-4)*. He has given us precious promises. He is mighty above all gods, therefore will we praise Him.

Psalms 18:3 - "I will call upon the Lord who is worthy to be praised: so shall I be saved from mine enemies."

3)   Praise is the God-ordained way of entering into His Presence. Praise is the gate that leads into His Presence *(Isaiah 62:10; Psalms 9:14; 22:3; 24:7, 9-10; 87:2; 118:19-21).*

Isaiah 60:18 - "Violence shall no more be heard in thy land, wasting nor destruction within thy borders; but thou shalt call thy walls Salvation, and thy gates Praise."

Psalms 100:4 - "Enter into his gates with thanksgiving, and into his courts with praise: be thankful unto him, and bless his name."

4)   Praise and worship are ways of glorifying God. We all want to glorify God and we all want God to be glorified. God is glorified by the one who praises Him.

Psalms 50:23 - "Whoso offereth praise glorifieth Me: and to him that ordereth his conversation aright will I shew the savlation of God."

5)   To praise the Lord is a good witness to others of the goodness of God. When Paul and Silas were in prison they were praising God *(Acts 16:25).* This was a tremendous witness to the jailor who knew just where to turn in a time of trouble. He went to the people who were praising God (See: *Isaiah 61:11).*

Psalms 40:3 - "And he hath put a new song in my mouth, even praise to our God: many shall see it, and fear, and shall trust in the Lord."

b)   We need to praise and worship God far more than He needs to receive it. From man's point of view praise is very beneficial.

1)   Praise and worship help us to become God-centered instead of self-centered. As we offer praise and worship unto God we are recognizing His Lordship and right to rule over us. We are humbling ourselves before God.

2)   Praise and worship are ways of staying our minds on Him *(Isaiah 26:3)*. As we stay our minds on God we will find a life of perfect peace.

3)   Praise and worship help us to develop our love relationship with God. Even in the natural as a husband and wife praise one another they are drawn closer to one another. In much the same way, when we praise the Lord we are drawn closer to Him. We are created to be love-beings to reciprocate God's love. As we praise and worship God we are fulfilling this calling.

4)   As we sow, we shall also reap *(Galatians 6:8)*. As we give, it shall be given unto us *(Luke 6:38)*. As we give ourselves to God, He, in turn, sends showers of blessing upon us *(Job 36:26-29)*. We don't want this to be the motive in our praising and worshipping God, but God does operate on the basis of principles. God has established the law of sowing and reaping.

5)   Praise and worship are faith in action. Praise and worship is the language of faith. When we believe and trust in God we will praise Him inspite of circumstances. A people of faith have set themselves (act of the will) to seek after the Lord.

6)   Praise and worship release the power and presence of God. In other words, God inhabits the praises of His people. Jehoshaphat found this out as he went singing into battle *(II Chronicles 20)*. Paul and Silas found out that as they sang praises to God the place was shaken *(Acts 16:25-26)*. God promises to be present in power as His people praise.

Psalms 22:3 - "But Thou art holy, O Thou that inhabitest the praises of Israel."

II Chronicles 5:13-14 - "It came even to pass, as the trumpeters and singers were as one, to make one sound to be heard in praising and thanking the Lord: and when they lifted up their voice with the trumpets and cymbals and instruments of music, and praised the Lord, saying, For He is good; for His mercy endureth forever: that then the house was filled with a cloud, even the house of the Lord; so that the priests could not stand to minister by reason of the cloud: for the glory of the Lord had filled the house of God."

7)   Praise and worship are directly related to a thankful heart. There are those who know God and yet do not glorify Him as God. These are unthankful *(Romans 1:21)*. As we praise God we come before His presence with thanksgiving which is always a good condition to receive the blessing of God *(Psalms 100:4)*.

8)   Praise and worship purify us. God wants a Church without spot or wrinkle. He has given several means whereby we might come to this place of sanctification. He has given us the washing of water by the Word *(Ephesians 5:26)*; He has given us prayer *(I Timothy 4:4-5)* and He has given us praise *(Proverbs 27:21)*.

9)   We are changed into the image of the one who we worship. If we are worshipping idols and things of our own hands we will be conformed to their image. If we have our eyes firmly fixed on the Lord Jesus Christ the author and finisher of our faith, we will ever be conformed to the image of the Son of God. Praise and worship are keys to this work of God in us.

Psalms 115:8 - "They that make them are like unto them; so is everyone that trusteth in them."

Psalms 106:19-20 - "They made a calf in Horeb, and worshipped the molten image. Thus they changed their glory into the similitude of an ox that eateth grass."

Romans 1:21-23 - "Because that, when they knew God, they glorified Him not as God, neither were thankful; but became vain in their imaginations, and their foolish heart was darkened. Professing themselves to be wise, they became fools, and changed the glory of the uncorruptible God into an image made like to corruptible man, and to birds, and fourfooted beasts, and creeping things."

II Corinthians 3:18 - "But we all, with open face beholding as in a glass the glory of the Lord, are changed into the same image from glory to glory, even as by the Spirit of the Lord."

10)   We have God's promise that He will meet with us and commune with us when we offer sacrifice unto the Lord *(Exodus 29:41-42)*. Many wonder why they never hear from God. Sometimes it is because they never put this principle of sacrifice into operation.

Worship is of extreme value in the life of the believer. Satan knew the value of worship and offered Christ the whole world if He would worship him *(Matthew 4:10)*. But Jesus let him know that worship belongs to God alone. As we worship God we will see restoration move at a tremendous pace.

57.   HOW ARE WE TO PRAISE THE LORD?

Paul exhorts us as believers to present our bodies a living sacrifice unto God *(Romans 12:10)*. He urges us to yield our members unto God as instruments of righteousness *(Romans 6:13)*. God wants to use all of our members to glorify God. He has given us expressions of praise and worship that involve our entire being.

As we give ourselves wholly to the worship of God we must remember that God wants us to worship Him IN SPIRIT and IN TRUTH. We are to worship Him in spirit by giving ourselves wholly unto Him. God does not want half-hearted efforts. He wants us to give our entire spirit to Him *(Psalms 111:1; 138:1-2)*.

Psalms 9:1 - "I will praise Thee, O Lord, with my whole heart; I will shew forth all Thy marvellous works."

Psalms 103:1 - "Bless the Lord, O my soul: and all that is within me bless His holy name."

God is not just interested in all of our energies being directed toward the worship of Him, but He wants us to worship Him in truth. He wants us to worship Him according to the Word of God *(John 17:17)*. As we worship on the basis of the Word we will know the truth which is able to set us free *(John 8:32)*. It will set us free from all our traditions that keep us from entering into true scriptural worship. Jesus said that it is traditions of men that will cancel the benefit of the Word of God.

Mark 7:7-8 - "Howbeit in vain do they worship me, teaching for doctrines the commandments of men. For laying aside the commandment of God, ye hold the tradition of men, as the washing of pots and cups: and many other such like things ye do."

Worship that is in truth is worship according to the Word of God. It is intelligent worship based on what God says about worship. If God spent so many chapters in the Old Testament telling His people exactly how they were to offer sacrifices unto Him, certainly God would also tell us in the Church how we are to worship Him. God never allowed His people the luxury of worshipping Him after the dictates of their own heart. More than once Israel got in trouble by doing what was right in their own eyes. We are to worship only at the dictates of God's Word.

> *John 4:23-24 - "But the hour cometh, and now is, when the true worshippers shall worship the Father in spirit and in truth: for the Father seeketh such to worship Him. God is a Spirit: and they that worship Him must worship Him in spirit and in truth."*

God has prescribed at least nine ways of worship in the Scripture that will totally involve us. Three ways involve the voice, three ways involve the hands, and three ways involve the body. We want to examine each of these areas and relate them to our life in the Church (refer to summary chart on the following page).

a)   THE MOUTH - God desires that we praise Him with our voice *(Psalms 42:4; 66:8)*. In doing this we will be using our mouth to make known the goodness of God. This may be through speaking and testimony, or it may be through song. God desires the words of our mouth to be that which is positive and inspiring to faith. When our words are words of faith, they are a praise unto God (See: *Psalms 40:3; 51:15; 63:5; 71:8, 15; 89:1; 145:21; 149:6; Romans 15;6).*

> *Psalms 109:30 - "I will greatly praise the Lord with my mouth; yea, I will praise Him among the multitude."*

b)   SINGING - The Scripture teaches that we are to come before His presence with singing *(Psalms 100:4)*. It has been said that you can tell the condition of a nation or even an individual by the songs that are sung. This is very true. Singing is a high expression of the inner

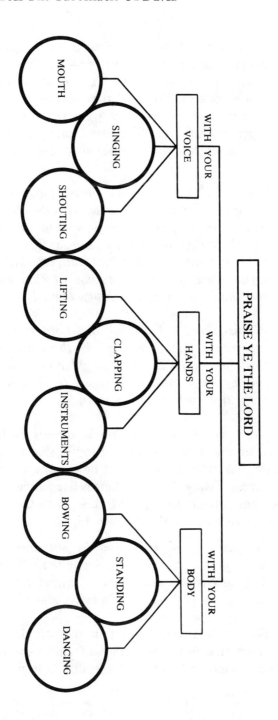

man: Loss of true spiritual singing is a sign of a people under judgement *(Isaiah 16:9-10)*. The Children of Israel were requested by their masters in Babylon to sing a song of Zion, but they had no song to sing in a strange land. When they were free from Babylonian captivity, however, they immediately took their harps off the willow trees and began to sing a new song unto God.

Psalms 137:1-4 - "By the rivers of Babylon, there we sat down, yea, we wept, when we remembered Zion. We hanged our harps upon the willows in the midst thereof. For there they that carried us away captive required of us a song; and they that wasted us, required of us mirth, saying, Sing us one of the songs of Zion. How shall we sing the Lord's song in a strange land?"

Psalms 126:1-2 - "When the Lord turned again the captivity of Zion, we were like them that dream. Then was our mouth filled with laughter, and our tongue with singing: then said they among the heathen, the Lord hath done great things for them."

These are days when God is turning captivities. It is no wonder that these are days of joyful singing. Every major visitation has birthed a wealth of new songs, the voice of joy and gladness. Today the same thing is happening. God's people are beginning to make a joyful noise unto the Lord, singing new songs unto the Lord *(Jeremiah 33:11)*.

Ephesians 5:18-19 - "And be not drunk with wine, wherein is excess; but be filled with the Spirit; speaking to yourselves in psalms and hymns and spiritual songs, singing and making melody in your heart to the Lord."

Singing is a very important ministry in the Church. Some think that music is merely a form of entertainment in the Church, and, sad to say, this is all it is in many churches.

Singing, however, is an act of worship and a ministry to the Body of Christ. There is a far higher purpose in song than entertainment. In fact, we are to teach and admonish one another in psalms and hymns and spiritual songs *(Colossians 3:16)*. Through singing we are able to teach and admonish. All music teaches and admonishes something. This is why it is so important to be sure that our songs and hymns and spiritual songs are scriptural in their content, for as we sing we are taught and admonished.

We can't help but notice that there are three realms of singing to be experienced by the Church: psalms, which were handed down to the early Church; hymns, which were very likely anointed compositions; and spiritual songs, which were possibly of a spontaneous nature. Spiritual singing would very likely include what the Old Testament refers to as a "new song" *(Psalms 33:3)*. It is wonderful to sing unto God the songs which He has given to others, but there is a special thrill when singing unto Him the song which He has put within your heart. The new song is given by the Spirit and is not a product of natural ability.

As we consider the subject of singing, we must also consider the place of choirs in the House of the Lord. In the Tabernacle of David, musicians were appointed or set aside for a special ministry of singing *(I Chronicles 15:16-22)*. Apparently David systematically appointed those who were to minister in the area of music and song, and a distinct charge was upon them for this. Jehoshaphat found out that singers were important in times of warfare. He appointed singers unto the Lord who were to praise *"the beauty of holiness, as they went out before the army."* This is the function of a choir, to lead the way into spiritual battle.

> *II Chronicles 20:21-22 - "And when he had consulted with the people, he appointed singers unto the Lord, and that should praise the beauty of holiness, as they went out before the army, and to say, Praise the Lord; for His mercy endureth forever. And when they began to sing and praise, the Lord set ambushments against the*

children of Ammon, Moab, and Mount Seir, which were
come against Judah; and they were smitten."

There are those in the House of God today whose ministry it is to lead into spiritual song and worship. Their ministry is to lead the congregation into the Presence of the Lord.
These singers lead the way into the gates of praise. As they do,
spiritual warfare is taking place. The enemy is being routed by
God who inhabits the praises of His people. When there is
warfare and the spiritual battle is hard, the singers should sing,
and God will send ambushments against the enemy. The
anointing will break the yoke. Great deliverance will take place
in the midst of the congregation WHILE they are singing and
worshipping the Lord.

In days of restoration, the singers are of particular importance. While the people were rebuilding the walls of Jerusalem singers were appointed to sing. This ministry of song was
as vital to them as the building of the wall. The singers were
given their portion as well as the workmen *(Nehemiah 11:23).*
The singers kept the word of their God *(Nehemiah 12:45),*
and they were appointed their portion of wine and oil with the
Levites *(Nehemiah 13:5).* Those who have a ministry in music
need to have the same anointing (wine and oil) upon them as
the congregation expects to be on those who minister in the
Word and other spiritual gifts and ministries. Music is not just
given to give someone a "job" in the Church.

The ministry of music is of tremendous importance in
the Church. The power that music has is almost incompre-
hensible. This is a generation filled with music. The music of
the day reflects the turmoil and frustration of its heart. The
song of the Church should reflect the peace, joy and content-
ment of the Christian life. A Church filled with joyful singing
is a Church filled with joyful Christians. Just as the songs of a
nation reflect its heartbeat even so the songs of the Church
reflect its relationship with God. The ministry of music cannot
be overemphasized, and the responsibility of each singer
cannot be overemphasized. The singers should be committed to
sing before the Lord *"with all their might"(I Chronicles 13:8).*

A ministry of this magnitude cannot be performed in a half-hearted way. The power and the glory of a united voice in song can be seen in the dedication of the Temple of Solomon *(II Chronicles 5:13)*. This should be a pattern for the New Testament Church in this hour. As the singers give themselves to the ministry of music in the House of the Lord we can expect the glory to descend in like manner.

See also: *Psalms 7:17; 9:2, 11; 18:49; 21:13; 27:6; 30:12; 47:6-7; 57:7; 61:8; 68:4, 32; 75:9; 92:1; 96:1; 104:33; 108:1, 3; 135:3; 138:1; 146:2; 147:1; Hebrews 2:12.*

c)   SHOUTING - It is easy to get the feeling that the worship in the Tabernacle of David was rather noisy at times. With the singers' singing with all their might and the musicians playing their instruments with all their might, it must have been quite a disturbance to those who didn't love the Lord. In addition to all of this, however, there was also shouting in the Tabernacle of David. If someone shouts at a football game no one gets too disturbed, in fact, they expect it; but some think it quite strange that there would be shouting in Church. The overall consequences of the greatest football game or the greatest play of that game will never reach beyond one year, while the effect of what God has done continues for eternity. That is something worth shouting about. All those who trust in the Lord will shout for joy *(Psalms 5:11)*. All those who are upright of heart will shout for joy *(Psalms 32:11)*. All those who favor the righteous cause will shout for joy and be glad *(Psalms 35:27)*, for God hath clothed them with salvation, and that is cause for rejoicing *(Psalms 132:9, 16)*.

Isaiah 12:6 - *"Cry out and shout, thou inhabitant of Zion: for great is the Holy One in the midst of thee."*

God is restoring the presence of the Lord in these days. When David recovered the Ark of the Covenant and was bringing it up to Jerusalem, there were great shouts for joy *(II Samuel 6:15)*. We can expect the same kind of rejoicing today!

d)   CLAPPING - It is God's desire that we clap as a sign of rejoicing *(Psalms 47:1)*. This may be while singing, but it may just be a separate offering, giving the Lord an applause. Men are so willing to show their acclaim to opera stars, entertainers and athletes. How much more worthy of our acclaim is God? We can show our pleasure in Him by clapping our hands in His presence (see: *Psalms 98:8, Isaiah 55:12)*.

e)   LIFTING OUR HANDS - A natural response for a grateful heart is to lift up one's hands before the Lord *(Lamentations 3:41)*. It is interesting that an uplifted hand is also a sign of having made an oath or covenant with God *(Genesis 14:22)*. We are a people who stand in covenant relationship with God and are grateful to the Lord for His lovingkindness toward us *(Psalms 63:3-4)*. Therefore we will lift up holy hands unto the Lord without wrath or doubting *(I Timothy 2:8)*.

Psalms 134 - "Behold, bless ye the Lord, all ye servants of the Lord, which by night stand in the house of the Lord. Lift up your hands in the sanctuary, and bless the Lord. The Lord that made heaven and earth bless thee out of Zion."

See also: *Psalms 28:2; 88:9; 119:48; 141:2; 143:6; Hebrews 12:12.*

f)   PLAYING INSTRUMENTS - Many people feel that the use of musical instruments in the Church has no New Testament authority. When we understand what God means when He says that He is going to rebuild the Tabernacle of David, we have no problem in this area. Paul exhorts the believers to use psalms on at least two occasions *(Ephesians 5:18-19; Colossians 3:16)*. The definition of the word "Psalm" is "an ode or song of praise accompanied by a harp or musical instrument." In the very definition of this word we have an exhortation to use musical instruments.

In the Tabernacle of David many instruments were used to enhance worship. In the Temple worship which followed there was singing and the use of instruments. For example when Hezekiah realized that God has extended his days and healed him, he wrote songs and appointed that they be sung *"to the stringed instruments all the days of our life in the House of the Lord" (Isaiah 38:20)*.

> *Psalms 150 - "Praise ye the Lord. Praise God in His sanctuary: praise Him in the firmament of His power. Praise Him for His mighty acts: praise Him according to His excellent greatness. Praise Him with the sound of the TRUMPET: praise Him with the PSALTERY and HARP. Praise Him with the TIMBREL and DANCE: praise Him with STRINGED INSTRUMENTS and ORGANS. Praise Him upon the loud CYMBALS: praise Him upon the high sounding CYMBALS. Let everything that hath breath praise the Lord. Praise ye the Lord."*

Those that have a ministry in music should wait on their ministry. In the Tabernacle worship there were those designated to *"prophesy with harps" (I Chronicles 25:1)*. Evidently the spirit of prophecy would come upon these minstrels and they would prophecy as they played. Those who play instruments should believe God for a prophetic touch to come upon them while they play their instruments. There have been occasions when a piano or organ has led in an anthem or worship and every other instrument has followed and played under the anointing, not one knowing what the musical "score" was. They were playing spontaneously under the anointing of the Holy Spirit forming an anthem of orchestral praise unto the

Lord. With such worship heaven must be filled!

At times we can see that it was a minstrel who set the mood or atmosphere for the prophetic anointing *(II Kings 3:15)*. We have found that Churches that have a strong emphasis in the area of music have no trouble maintaining a heavy anointing and a constant flow of Body ministry. Music does create an atmosphere. The world knows it and misuses it, but we want to use music to draw people into the presence of God.

The Scripture clearly places a stern requirement on the individual who desires to minister on his instrument in the House of the Lord. The one who plays is to play skillfully *(Psalms 33:3; Ezekiel 33:32)*. There is no premium on ignorance in the things of God. Rigorous training in the playing of an instrument is a great asset to the worship in the House of the Lord. The House of God is not a place of practice. When unskilled musicians lead worship, it can only bring disorder to the corporate expression. However, when skill is coupled with the anointing of God dynamic things can take place in the realm of worship. Because of David's skill on his harp, the evil spirit was driven from Saul *(I Samuel 16:17)*. It wasn't merely his skill, however, but it was his skill plus the anointing of God.

g)   STANDING - There is a place for standing before the Lord in praise to Him *(Psalms 134:1)*. About the only position that is not mentioned in the *Psalms* in connection with worship is sitting. It is difficult to really get involved in worshipping the Lord in a seated position. As we stand in His presence we are giving Him glory, reverance and awe. When a judge walks into a court room everyone stands to their feet. We are in the presence of THE Judge. It is more than appropriate to stand before Him.

    Psalms 135:1-2 - "Praise ye the Lord. Praise ye the name of the Lord; praise Him, O ye servants of the Lord. Ye that stand in the House of the Lord, in the courts of the House of our God."

h) BOWING OR KNEELING - When Solomon typically presented himself as a living sacrifice in the presence of the people, he knelt down, stretched forth his hands toward heaven and cried unto God *(II Chronicles 6: 13-14).* Kneeling or bowing is a gesture of humility on our part. When we fully recognize the magnificence of the One before whom we gather, it is not surprising that we should kneel.

Psalms 95:6 - "O come, let us worship and bow down: let us kneel before the Lord our Maker."

i) DANCING - Not many people deny that we should stand in the presence of God, but standing is only mentioned twice in the *Psalms.* Not many people would question the validity of kneeling in the House of God, even though kneeling is only mentioned once in the *Psalms.* But when it comes to dancing, which is mentioned three times in the *Psalms,* a red flag goes up. Sometimes we are so used to seeing how the devil has perverted a thing that we loose a desire for the true expression of that thing. When we think of dancing, we automatically think of that carnal expression of dance which is found in the world. The Bible does say that we are to praise the Lord in the dance. If this is true, we should want to know just how we can do the Word of God.

Psalms 149:3 - "Let them praise His name in the dance: let them sing praises unto Him with the timbrel and harp."

Psalms 150:4 - "Praise Him with the timbrel and dance: praise Him with stringed instruments and organs."

It should be noted that the phrase "dancing in the spirit" cannot be found in the Word of God. This is a phrase which has been coined by those who have not understood the full message of praise and the sacrifice of praise. Every act of faith in worship involves a sacrifice on the part of the worshipper. The lifting of hands, clapping, singing and shouting are all conscious acts that are done on the basis of an understanding of the Word of God and a willingness to obey its dictates. Dancing before the Lord is no different. You don't have to get a special quickening to sing, and you don't have to get a special quickening to dance.

"Dancing before the Lord" or "spiritual dancing" is worship on a very high plain and should always be considered and treated as such. It is not merely an "emotional release" as some have said. Truly God does and always will come down to satisfy the emotional needs of His people, but the primary purpose in this aspect of worship is obedience to the known will of God through our worship.

It should be kept in mind that dancing has been an integral part of the worship pattern of every society and culture down through the ages. It is no wonder that in this last generation it has become something so degraded and filthy, for as sin reaches its height, Satan will take everything which has once been a part of true spiritual worship and drag it to its lowest depths. This is why God is restoring the dance to the last day Church. One of the ultimate expressions of worship in the believer's life is the total abandonment of strength until God completely possesses us spirit, soul and body. Whatever gods the heathen may worship, there is to be found somewhere in that worship the expression of dance. This indicates that there is born in the heart of every man a great desire to abandon himself in the worship of his god. How much more should we abandon ourselves with all that is in us unto THE LIVING GOD.

God is restoring joy to the Church -- a joy which has never before been made manifest. He wants us to come to the place of fulness of joy to be found in the "joy of the harvest." Dancing is a vital expression of this joy. There is, however, an order to God's restoration that acts as a safeguard in this area.

Jeremiah 31:12-13 - "Therefore they shall come and sing in the height of Zion, and shall flow together to the goodness of the Lord, for wheat, and for wine, and for oil, and for the young of the flock and of the herd: and their soul shall be as a watered garden; and they shall not sorrow any more at all. Then shall the virgin rejoice in the dance, both young men and old together: for I will turn their mourning into joy, and will comfort them, and make them rejoice from their sorrow."

Jeremiah gives us the three ingredients that are able to keep us in balance. First God will restore the Word (wheat), for everything must be founded on the basis of the revealed Word of God. Second, God restores the joy of the Lord (wine). When the Word of God and the joy of the Lord meet up with the third ingredient, the anointing (oil), then shall the Church (virgin) rejoice in the dance. When the foundation has been properly laid in the Word of God, the expression in the dance can follow.

Times of visitation and deliverance have always been characterized by the expression of dancing. When Israel was delivered from Egyptian bondage, Miriam led the women of Israel in the dance *(Exodus 15:21).* When David brought up the Ark of the Covenant, he laid aside all his kingly robes, clothed himself with a linen ephod which was the garment of the priest and danced before the Lord *(II Samuel 6:14).* When God restores a people as He is doing with the Church there is dancing that springs forth *(Jeremiah 31:4).* Even when God turns an individual's personal captivity of depression and mourning, a natural response is to dance, skip or leap for joy before the Lord.

Psalms 30:11 - "Thou hast turned for me my mourning into dancing: thou hast put off my sack cloth, and girded me with gladness."

In the New Testament we find the same response to a turned captivity. In *Isaiah* it was prophesied that the lame man would leap as the hart, and in *Acts* this was literally fulfilled *(Isaiah 35:6; Acts 3)*. It must have caused some commotion in that day when a man who had sat for years in the same spot, begging for alms, having crippled legs, watching the religious leaders of his day going in and out of the house of God never having the answer to his need, suddenly come leaping into the Temple praising God. There were possibly many people who thought it a little undignified, but the lame man must have felt it quite appropriate. Many have wondered why, in this visitation of the Holy Spirit, we are so zealous about our worship. The answer is found in this account. For years many of us have sat and watched as ministers came and went in our churches. For years we listened to sermons without having our own personal needs met to such an extent that we could enter in and become part of what God was doing. For years the cry went up from our hearts, "Oh God, is this all there is for us?" Then, in His mercy, God brought ministry our way who gave us more than we asked for, and we received strength where we thought we would never have strength. God has, in fact, done so abundantly more than we asked that we are caused to leap for joy and shout praise unto God.

Before we conclude this subject, it is necessary to mention some areas of caution when it comes to spiritual dancing.

1)   This expression should be initiated by leadership. Even as Miriam led the women and David led the nation, the leadership should lead the people of God in worship. It is never right for *"every man to do that which is right in his own eyes."* In times of rejoicing there should be leadership for the people of God. Lack of leadership has caused much of the reproach which exists today toward this move of God. There is not one thing wrong with truth, but without leadership to administrate the truth, lack of wisdom can and does cause much reproach. God's people have been brought out from under the rod of the oppressor, and for this reason there is great rejoicing in the camp!

2)   Spiritual dancing is not a matter of individual expres-

sion, but it is a Body function. Spiritual dancing is not new. The Pentecostal revival saw much expression of praise in the dance in its early years. The "new" aspect of this truth is an understanding of the teaching of the Word of God and the knowledge that this is not just an individual expression, but rather, when the Spirit moves upon the congregation with joy and rejoicing, God's highest order is that the whole congregation move as one Body in this expression of Worship. With the revelation of the truths of the Body of Christ and Body worship has come the understanding that God wants each member to submerge himself in the activities of the whole Body in worship. When there is a clapping, we all clap; when there is lifting up of hands, we all participate; and when there is dancing, God's order is that the whole Body participate in this expression of Worship.

3) We must not prescribe a given mode of expression in this area to the exclusion of others. Always keep in mind that God expresses Himself through each individual in a different manner. Just as we have differences in personality, even so there will be a variation in the expression of God from each member. Therefore, it is wrong to expect all to worship God in dancing in exactly the same way. Some may "whirl violently about" as David did before the Ark. Others may "skip or leap about" as the lame man who received healing. Others may "dance with a measured step" as the original implies. Whatever the case there is an abandonment to God in worship, and the Scripture indicates that this is pleasing to God.

4) As with all the things of God, dancing should not become a mere form. Dancing is an extreme form of worship. Care should be taken not to overdo or make common something which is intended to be holy and pure. That is, in one sense, a dangerous truth, for the carnal flesh can easily take something such as this and cause it to become an offense to new converts and those coming into the Church for the first time.

5)   It is important for us not to despise what God has
      ordained. The elder son was disturbed by the dancing
      over the lost son's return *(Luke 15:25)*. Michael, the
      daughter of Saul (flesh), despised David for this open
      display of worship. Michael was severely judged of the
      Lord for her attitude. She was made barren. This should
      be a solemn warning to God's people today. Judgment
      comes on those who despise the anointing, but blessing
      comes to those who receive it and appreciate what God
      has done. The spirit of Michael is still in the Church
      today, but those who are clothed with the robes of
      priesthood will still sing and rejoice in the Lord for the
      Ark is coming *(I Chronicles 15:10, 27-28)*.

58.   WHEN SHOULD WE PRAISE AND WORSHIP GOD?

The *Psalms* teach us that we are to praise God every day
(Psalms 145:2), seven times a day *(Psalms 119:164)*.
In other words we are to praise Him at all times *(Psalms
34:1)*. This is to continue forever or as long as we have
being *(Psalms 45:17; 104:33; 146:1-3)*. This is one thing
that we can expect to do for eternity.

*Psalms 34:1 - "I will bless the Lord at all times: His
praise shall continually be in my mouth."*

*Psalms 113:1-3 - "Praise ye the Lord. Praise, O ye ser-
vants of the Lord, praise the name of the Lord. Blessed
be the name of the Lord from this time forth and for-
evermore. From the rising of the sun unto the going
down of the same the Lord's name is to be praised."*

59.   WHERE SHOULD WE PRAISE AND WORSHIP THE LORD?

We are certainly to praise God wherever we may find
ourselves in our daily Christian walk, but there are also
times when it is important for us to gather and offer a

corporate expression of worship unto God *(Psalms 22: 25; 108:3; 134:2; 138:1-2)*.

Psalms 35:18 - "I will give Thee thanks in the great congregation: I will praise Thee among much people."

Psalms 111:1 - "Praise ye the Lord. I will praise the Lord with my whole heart, in the assembly of the upright, and in the congregation."

60.   WHO SHOULD PRAISE AND WORSHIP THE LORD?

The Scripture gives various categories of people who are to praise the Lord. The complete list is sufficient to include everyone.

a)   The heaven and the earth are to praise the Lord *(Psalms 69:34; 89:5)*. All creation is included under this category.

b)   All the nations and all the people are to praise God *(Psalms 117:1)*.

c)   The poor and the needy are to praise God *(Psalms 74:21)*. We should never let circumstances rob us of praise.

d)   All the servants of the Lord are to praise God *(Psalms 134:1; 113:1; 103:21)*. This would include all of those who fear the Lord *(Psalms 22:23, 26)*. If we truly fear the Lord we will have a desire to honor Him with our praise. The characteristic of saints is that they shout for joy *(Psalms 132:9; 145:10)*.

e)   In fact, everything that has breath is to praise the Lord *(Psalms 150:6)*. The very fact that we praise is a sign of life. It is the living that praise the Lord *(Isaiah 38:19)*, for the dead, or those who have returned to dust do not praise the Lord *(Psalms 115:17; 30:9; 88:10-11; Isaiah 38:18)*.

As we can see praise is for everyone. It requires a whole body (the Local Church) to worship. This is not an activity for five or ten per cent of the congregation *(Mark 12:30)*. Praise and worship is an entire body function.

> *Psalms 117 - "O praise the Lord, all ye nations: praise Him all ye people. For His merciful kindness is great toward us: and the truth of the Lord endureth forever. Praise ye the Lord."*

61. WHAT DISTINCTION CAN WE MAKE BETWEEN PRAISE AND WORSHIP?

The best way to distinguish between these two concepts is to study the etymology of the words that are used in the Old Testament and the New Testament for each of these. We offer the following outline:

a) WORSHIP

    1) In the Old Testament two primary words are used.

        a) Abodah - This is a general word usually translated "labour, work, ministry or service of God."

        b) Shachah - This word is used to describe the specific act of worship. It means to bow, prostrate oneself in homage or proceed humbly.

    2) In the New Testament we also have the same distinction maintained.

        a) Latruo - This is the general word originally meaning servitude – the state of a hired labourer or slave, and thence the service of God -- divine worship.

        b) Proskuneo - This corresponds to the Hebrew word describing the specific act of worship. It means to prostrate oneself, to adore, to bow down or to worship.

It is not difficult for us to see the two-fold meaning of the word "worship." In the general sense, all that we do in service to our God, all that we do in the name of the Lord, all that we do because of our commitment to Him could be called worship. This is the pure religion that James referred to *(1:27)*. But, on the other hand, there is a specific act of worship where we humble ourselves before God. We prostrate ourselves in reverence and awe at His greatness. Worship proceeds from the heart of the one who fears the Lord. Jesus knew that both aspects of worship were important. He knew that our whole life must be an expression of worship, and, yet, we must have specific times where we just give all our attention to Him. As Christ was being tempted, He reminded Satan, *"Thou shalt worship (proskuneo) the Lord thy God, and Him only shalt thou serve (latruo)" Luke 4:8.*

b)   PRAISE

     1)   In the Old Testament there are three primary roots that are translated "praise."

         a)   Yadah - This word in the primary root means to throw or cast. It came to mean a rendering of thanks in worship primarily because of the use of the hands in praise unto God. Therefore the word origin implies a praise to God with hands extended.

         b)   Halal - Some of the original meanings of this word include to shout for joy, rejoice, cry aloud, and implore. It has come to mean to boast, to make show, to rave or to celebrate. This implies that we are audibly to boast in the Lord.

         c)   Shaback - This word means to laud, praise or address in a loud tone. It is not difficult to see why the Tabernacle filled with praise was a noisy place.

     2)   In the New Testament we have only one root word in regard to praise, "aineo." This word is simply used to mean praise to God.

We have to say that praise is worship in a general sense. But praise is specifically that act of worship or service unto God in which we audibly render thanks to God with the lifting up of our hands. Worship in the specific sense involves a humble adoration, a bowing of the spirit before the Almighty God. God desires both. He delights in the praises, the boasting, the celebrating of His people, but He also desires that we bow before Him.

The Church is to be a worshipping community, but it is also to be a place of praise. God is at the present time restoring praise to the Church. He is getting the Church ready for the Second Coming of Christ. Before Christ can come again, praise must be fully restored as spoken by the prophets *(Acts 3:21; Jeremiah 33:11)*. In the last days God will give us a garment of praise *(Isaiah 61:3)*. This indicates that praise is not to be a once-in-awhile experience, but it is a garment which is to be worn by the end-time Church. This garment is the perfect answer for depression which is so common in this generation. No nervous condition or depression can stand in the presence of one who wears the garment of praise. It will be with the high praises of God in our mouth that we will conquer all our enemies, even the last enemy—death *(Hebrews 9:27)*.

> *Psalms 149:6-9 - "Let the high praises of God be in their mouth, and a two-edged sword in their hand; to execute vengeance upon the heathen, and punishments upon the people; to bind their kings with chains, and their nobles with fetters of iron; to execute upon them the judgment written: this honour have all His saints. Praise ye the Lord."*

The gates of Zion (the Church) are referred to many times as praise *(Isaiah 60:18)*. We are encouraged to go through the gates of praise to prepare the way of the Lord *(Isaiah 62:10-12)*. Through praise we enter into the gate of

God's presence. Through praise we enter into a life of victory. Through praise we enter into ministry unto the Lord. For this reason *"the Lord loveth the gates of Zion more than all the dwellings of Jacob" (Psalms 87:2)*. Our Lord Jesus Christ is the Lion of the tribe of Judah. "Judah" means praise. Christ is captain over a host of people who know the importance of praise. Let us diligently pursue after this important aspect of worship. Let us not allow our past traditions to make the Word of God of none effect!

STUDY QUESTIONS FOR CHAPTER TEN

1. Describe the Tabernacle of David.

2. How can we relate the Tabernacle of David to the Church?

3. How does each piece of furniture in the Tabernacle of Moses relate to our experience in Christ?

4. How did the order of worship in the Tabernacle of David differ from that found in the Tabernacle of Moses?

5. On what mountain was the Tabernacle of David erected?

6. What is the key to understanding the Tabernacle of David?

7. List ten reasons why we praise God.

8. List nine ways in which we are to praise God.

9. Why is music so important in the Church?

10. How do we know that we are to use instruments in the New Testament Church?

11. What are four cautions in regard to spiritual dancing?

12. When should we praise the Lord?

13. Where should we praise theLord?

14. Who is to praise the Lord?

15. Define worship.

16. Define praise.

CHAPTER ELEVEN

*God's Eternal Purpose
In The Church*

God's Eternal
Purpose In
The Church
Chapter Eleven

God is doing some tremendous things in these days. By now it should be clear that the plan and purpose of God culminates in the Church *(Ephesians 3:10-11)*. As the end of all things draws near, we can expect that God is going to do something in the Church that staggers our imaginations *(Ephesians 4:11-16)*. These are exciting days and God does not want us to be ignorant of His plans and purposes. For this reason He has given us the Word of God which is able to make us wise unto salvation. He has given us the Old Testament which gives us the history of the Church in picture language. He has given us the New Testament which lays down the principles for entering into the Kingdom and the fulness of what God has for us. If this is true, we can expect that all that God has done and all that He will yet do is pictured in the Old Testament, just waiting for our discovery. It may be hidden from the natural eye, but is our honour to search out the glorious truths which God has hidden for the seeker in His Word *(Proverbs 25:2)*.

In the Tabernacle of Moses we have a beautiful picture of what God is doing in terms of restoration (see chart on the following page). Man's approach to God began at the gate. The gate speaks to us of the Lord Jesus Christ as the only way to salvation. Just inside the gate was the Brazen Altar upon which the animals were offered for the sins of the people. In the experience of the Church, the Brazen Altar was restored in the time of Martin Luther when he received the truth of salvation by faith in the sacrifice of the Lamb of God.

The Brazen Laver was the next piece of furniture to be experienced. The Laver was used for washing or cleansing for

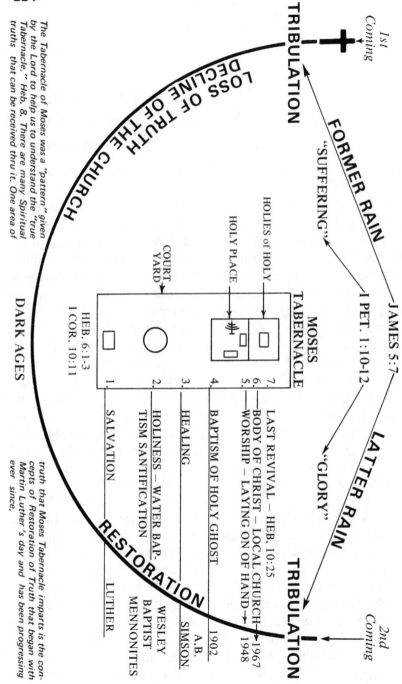

1st Coming

TRIBULATION

FORMER RAIN

"SUFFERING"

JAMES 5:7

I PET. 1:10-12

"GLORY"

LATTER RAIN

TRIBULATION

2nd Coming

LOSS OF TRUTH DECLINE OF THE CHURCH

DARK AGES

RESTORATION

MOSES TABERNACLE

COURT YARD

HOLY PLACE

HOLIES of HOLY

HEB. 6:1-3
I COR. 10:11

1. SALVATION — LUTHER
2. HOLINESS — WATER BAP-TISM SANTIFICATION — WESLEY BAPTIST MENNONITES
3. HEALING — A.B. SIMSON
4. BAPTISM OF HOLY GHOST — 1902
5. WORSHIP — LAYING ON OF HAND — 1948
6. BODY OF CHRIST — LOCAL CHURCH — 1967
7. LAST REVIVAL — HEB. 10:25

The Tabernacle of Moses was a "pattern" given by the Lord to help us to understand the "true Tabernacle." Heb. 8. There are many Spiritual truths that can be received thru it. One area of

truth that Moses Tabernacle imparts is the concepts of Restoration of Truth that began with Martin Luther's day and has been progressing ever since.

both the priests and the sacrifices. This washing of water was required by God for any and all ministry. The Laver speaks to us of the restoration of both water baptism which has the effect of washing away sins *(Acts 22:16)* and an emphasis on the Word of God in holiness *(Ephesians 5:26).*

As the priest desired to minister in the Sanctuary in the Holy Place, he had to enter into the door. At this time he had to change his garments before entering in. This change of garments prior to entering into some of the mysteries or secret things of God speaks to us of the Baptism of the Holy Spirit. As we are baptized with the Spirit we are endued or actually "clothed" with power from on high. It is this clothing that brings us into the light of His Word (The Candlestick). It is at this point that the eyes of our understanding are enlightened.

Once inside the door the priest was able to minister at the Candlestick, the Table of Shewbread and the Altar of Incense. Since the restoration of the laying on of hands God has given a special quickening and revelation to the Word of God. The Candlestick with its 66 ornaments can represent the Word of God. As we minister in the light of the Candlestick God opens His truth to us. The secret is in the oil in the lamps. God has poured out the oil of the Spirit which has made the light of the Word shine bright *(Psalms 119:105, 130).* People no longer go to the Bible as a history book, but as a great treasure field, ready to give up its wealth to those who search and dig diligently.

God has also been emphasizing the life and health that can be ours in connection with the Table of the Lord. The Table of Shewbread upheld the bread that was to be eaten by the priests before the Lord. Upon this bread there was to be frankincense which had medicinal properties. Wine was also used in connection with the bread. In the New Testament, Jesus interprets the bread as being His body. He is the Bread of Life, and His life is imparted in the eating of Him *(John 6: 53-57).* God is still adding dimension to this truth as we minister as priests before Him.

One of the clearest messages for us in this context is in

connection with the Golden Altar of Incense. The Altar of Incense was placed in the Holy Place immediately in front of the veil. This veil was the only thing that separated the Altar of Incense from the Ark of the Covenant *(Exodus 30:1-10; 40:26-27)*. We could say that positionally it was the last piece of furniture one experienced before reaching that which was within the veil. The Altar of Incense speaks strongly of the prayers and worship of the saints *(Revelations 8:1-5; 5:8)*. It was here that the evening sacrifice was offered *(Psalms 141:2)*. These are days when God is causing the incense to ascend in the form of prayer and praise. This incense will be foundational to that Great Day which is to follow.

The Tabernacle picture does not end at the Altar of Incense. One thing that the message of restoration has shown us is God's purpose and working throughout Church history. But His working and purpose extend beyond the past. The message of restoration leaves us with a challenge to go on to enter into what God has for us on the road ahead. In the ministry of the Tabernacle of Moses there was no day like the Great Day of Atonement when the High Priest entered in beyond the veil into the presence of God. This was a tremendous day of rejoicing when sin was taken out of the camp. As the High Priest entered into that within the veil, we cannot help but notice that he entered swinging the censer in a cloud of incense *(Leviticus 16:12-14)*. As we enter further into what God has for us, we, too, must enter in a cloud of prayer and praise.

There is something more for the People of God. Many would tend to get lax in spiritual matters waiting for the coming of the Lord. We believe with men of God around the world that we are living in the glorious climax of the Ages. What can we expect? What is our part and responsibility at the end of the Age? Are we just to wait for a secret rapture to take us all away? Will the Church grow weaker and smaller until there is just God's "little flock" left? NO! Absolutely not! For nearly five hundred years the Lord has been bringing back (restoring) truth to the Church, and He continues to do so even in the present day. Certainly any believer with spiritual eyes can see that we have been in the process of receiving truth, line upon line and precept upon precept. And for what purpose? Is it because God is having fun with us? NO! God is doing all of this that He might present to His Son a glorious (glory-us) bride without spot or wrinkle!

62.   **WHAT CAN WE EXPECT IN THE FUTURE FOR THE CHURCH?**

We can expect to see the Church become stronger and stronger in the earth *(Numbers 14:21; Habakkuk 2:14)*. The Church will become a powerful, redemptive force in society, becoming the *"salt of the earth", "the light of the world"* and a *"city set on an hill. . ." (Matthew 5: 13-14)*. As God's people stand for righteousness and godliness against the flood tide of the enemy, we are going to see confrontation take place, a spiritual battle for the hearts of men. But the Church, in her strength and glory will prevail *(Matthew 16:18)*. The house of God will be exalted *(Isaiah 2:2)*, and will have an effect for righteousness upon society and government and the nations of the earth *(Isaiah 60:1-5)*. We will see the people of God once again exercise dominion over the earth *(Genesis 1:26-28; Psalms 149)*.

Paul tells us that God put all things under the feet of Christ *(Ephesians 1:22)*. Just as dominon was given to the first Adam, dominion has been restored in the last Adam. Now we are the Body of Christ, and we too are to have all things in subjection to us. At the present time we don't see this reality with the natural eye. But the day is coming when we will be full partakers of Christ's dominion *(Hebrews 2:6-15)*. God is waiting until all the enemies of Christ are put under His feet. The last enemy to be destroyed is death. There will be a generation of people created in the last days who will break their appointment with death *(Psalms 102:18)*. This will be a people not just fortunate enough to be alive at His coming, but a people of faith who are willing to act in faith and respond positively to all that God says. It will be a people of praise who walk by faith and not by sight. God has given us the weapon of praise to deal with the enemy. God has given us spiritual weapons to fight spiritual battles *(II Corinthians 10:4)*. Now is the time to practice using the weapons with which we will face the enemy of death. We will have no time to get our weapons in working order at the midnight hour *(Matthew 25:1-10)*.

> *Isaiah 43:18-21 - "Remember not the former things, neither consider the things of old. Behold I will do a new thing; now it shall spring forth; shall ye not know it? I will even make a way in the wilderness, and rivers in the desert. The beast of the field shall honor me, the jackals and the owls, because I give waters in the wilderness, and rivers in the desert, to give drink to my people, my chosen. This people have I formed for myself; they shall show forth my praise."*

63.   WHAT ARE THREE KEYS TO VISITATION?

There are many Churches who have not yet tasted the fruit of this land. There are some Churches that have only a foretaste of what it can be like. Some Churches are camped around the Brazen Altar. Some are encamped about the Brazen Laver of Water Baptism. All of these things are good, but God wants us ALL to move into the fulness of what He has for us. Everyone who is honest must admit that no one has experienced all of that fulness. Therefore, wherever we are, we are all still in need of further revelation and visitation. If we want God to bring visitation to the Church, there are certain keys that are essential in these days. As we use the keys we can expect God to open His Word to us. There are at least three essential keys to every visitation.

a)   PRAISE - We have already mentioned the importance of praise. Praise is an act of faith which releases the power and presence of God. There can be no visitation without the power and presence of God *(Psalms 22:3)*.

b)   PRAYER - Prayer is that which waters revival. Prayer is that incense that ascends before the throne of God. It is a sweet smelling savor in the nostrils of God *(Proverbs 15:8)*. Prayer is part of our spiritual armour, and it is, therefore, essential in times of spiritual battle *(Epheisans 6:18)*. The Scripture demonstrates many times that prayer is essential prior to any visitation by God. The birth of Samuel in a time of darkness was the result of prayer *(I Samuel 1:10, 12; 2:1)*. The first coming of the Lord was preceded by the prayers of the faithful *(Luke 2:25, 37)*. Prayer was essential to the coming of the Spirit on Pentecost *(Acts 1:14)*. The visitation at the house of Cornelius was due to previous prayer and fasting *(Acts 10:30)*. Peter was delivered from prison because of the prayers of the faithful *(Acts 12:5-13)*. Prayer is a tremendous force that God has given us to change situations and move mountains.

Just as prayer has been important for every other visitation, prayer is essential to THIS visitation. God has revealed His intention to build a House, we need to set ourselves to seek the Lord *(II Samuel 7:27)*. God's House is to be a House of Prayer *(Luke 19:46)*. As the people of God, we need to give God no rest until He establishes Zion as a praise in the earth *(Isaiah 62:6-7)*. Solomon knew this key in his early life. He knew when God's people were put to the worse before the enemy; when the heaven was shut up, and there was no rain; and when there was dearth in the land, if God's people would humble themselves and turn to the Lord in prayer that God would heal them *(II Chronicles 6:24-30; 7:14)*. All these conditions apply spiritually today. God's people have been put to the worse before the enemy. There have been times of spiritual drought. There has been spiritual dearth in the land. We need to give ourselves to prayer. We have God's promise in these days that God *"will regard the prayer of the destitute, and not despise their prayer" (Psalms 102:17)*.

c)   UNITY - In every previous period of restoration and
        visitation God has singled out individuals to use as His
        instrument or voice. He used men like Luther and Wes-
        ley and others. Every visitation requires a vehicle to be
        used of God. The beautiful thing that God is doing in
        these days is that He is presently using the vehicle of
        His Body, the "collective," corporate Church. God is
        not magnifying any particular man, but He is sovereign-
        ly moving throughout His Body world-wide. This places
        a heavy responsibility on us for we cannot be effective
        if we are pulling against one another. It was only as the
        early Church was in *"one place"* and *"in one accord"*
        that the Holy Spirit fell upon them. There are many
        congregations today that have correct doctrinal truths
        but still no visitation. They wonder why, when every
        member is pulling against another. The writings of Paul
        constantly contain strong warnings and corrections
        about division and strife *(I Corinthians 1:10; 3)*. Paul
        knew that strife would cause them to miss their day of
        visitation. The Local Church is the wine skin, and it
        must not be rent *(Luke 5:36-39)*.

    The key to unity is a revelation of the Body of Christ.
Deeper truth and greater revelation have little or no value unless we have an understanding of the Body of Christ. When a
Local Church understands the revelation of the Body of
Christ, they will no longer allow themselves to be involved
in gossip, backbiting, slander, talebearing, or whispering, for
when they attack the Body they are attacking the person of
Jesus Christ *(Matthew 25:34-46)*. The opposite of gossip and
slander will be instrumental in bringing unity to the Body. The
ever-progressing revelation of praise and worship is one of the
greatest factors in the unifying of the Body of Christ. When we
are all truly worshipping Jesus and praising His name, there
can be no division.
    As we examine the theme of unity in the Scripture its
importance is evident.

1)   Unity was the atmosphere on the Day of Pente-
      cost.

      *Acts 1:14 - "These all continued with one accord
      in prayer and supplication, with the women, and
      Mary the mother of Jesus, and with his brethren."*

      *Acts 2:1 - ". . .and when the day of Pentecost was
      fully come, they were all with one accord in one
      place."*

2)   Unity was a key message of the prophets of old.
      They prophesied that *"in that day"* the people of
      God would *"see eye to eye"* and *"flow together."*

      *Joel 2:7-8 - "They shall run like mighty men;
      they shall climb the wall like men of war; and
      they shall march every one on his ways, and they
      shall not break their ranks: Neither shall one
      thrust another; they shall walk every one in his
      path: and when they fall upon the sword, they
      shall not be wounded."*

      *Joel 2:23-27 - "Be glad then, ye children of Zion,
      and rejoice in the Lord your God: for he hath
      given you the former rain moderately, and he will
      cause to come down for you the rain, the former
      rain, and the latter rain in the first month. And
      the floors shall be full of wheat, and the vats
      shall overflow with wine and oil. And I will re-
      store to you the years that the locust hath eaten,
      the cankerworm, and the caterpiller, and the
      palmerworm, my great army which I sent among
      you. And ye shall eat in plenty, and be satisifed,
      and praise the name of the Lord your God, that
      hath dealt wondrously with you: and my people*

*shall never be ashamed. And ye shall know that
I am in the midst of Israel, and that I am the Lord
your God, and none else: and my people shall
never be ashamed."*

*Isaiah 52:7-8 - "How beautiful upon the mount-
ains are the feet of him that bringeth good tidings, that publisheth peace; that bringeth good
tidings of good, that publisheth salvation; that
saith unto Zion, Thy God reigneth! Thy watchmen shall lift up the voice; with the voice together shall they sing: for they shall see eye to eye,
when the Lord shall bring again Zion."*

*Isaiah 60:1-5 - "Arise, shine; for thy light is come,
and the glory of the Lord is risen upon thee. For,
behold, the darkness shall cover the earth, and
gross darkness the people: but the Lord shall
arise upon thee, and his glory shall be seen upon
thee. And the Gentiles shall come to thy light,
and kings to the brightness of thy rising. Lift up
thine eyes round about, and see: all they gather
themselves together, they come to thee: thy sons
shall come from far, and thy daughters shall be
nursed at thy side. Then thou shalt see, and flow
together, and thine heart shall fear, and be en-
larged; because the abundance of the sea shall be
converted unto thee, the forces of the Gentiles
shall come unto thee."*

3)   Unity was a major factor in the Prayer of Jesus.

*John 17:21-22 - "That they all may be one; as
thou, Father, art in me, and I in thee, that they
also may be one in us: that the world may believe
that thou has sent me. And the glory which thou
gavest me I have given them; that they may be
one, even as we are one."*

4)   It will be witness to the world in so much that it will cause them to believe *(Psalms 133; John 17: 21-22)*.

5)   Unity is the condition in which the new wine is found. The new wine speaks of the whole message of restoration. This message thrives in the *"cluster."*

> *Isaiah 65:8 - "Thus saith the Lord, As the new wine is found in the cluster, and one saith, Destroy it not; for a blessing is in it: so will I do for my servants' sakes, that I may not destroy them all."*

6)   Unity is a requirement for any body, natural or spiritual, to function properly.

As the Church abandons all battles within the Body of Christ and begins to unite around the Lord Jesus Christ we can expect great things to happen. Unity is a tremendously powerful force, even in the world *(Genesis 11)*. No enemy will be able to stand before a body of people standing in true spiritual unity in Christ Jesus. True spiritual unity carries with it many rewards which are summed up for us in *Psalms 133*.

> *Psalms 133 - "Behold, how good and how pleasant it is for brethren to dwell together in unity! It is like the precious ointment upon the head, that ran down upon the beard, even Aaron's beard: that went down to the skirts of his garments; As the dew of Hermon, and as the dew that descended upon the mountains of Zion: for there the Lord commanded the blessing, even life forevermore.*

1)   Unity brings the anointing upon the whole congregation. As we stand in Christ, in that Body-unity, we partake of the anointing that is poured upon the Head, the Lord Jesus Christ.

2)   Unity makes available the dew of heaven. The earth was
       formerly watered by the dew. It was watered from with-
       in *(Genesis 2:5-6)*. This is the ideal for all believers that
       they be watered from within *(John 7:38-39)*.

3)   In the condition or atmosphere of unity God commands
       the blessing, even life forevermore. Where the Lord
       commands life, there can be no death.

> *Romans 12:4-16 - "For as we have many members in
> one body, and all members have not the same office:
> So we, being many, are one body in Christ, and every
> one members one of another. Having then gifts differ-
> ing according to the grace that is given to us, whether
> prophecy, let us prophesy according to the proportion
> of faith; Or ministry, let us wait on our ministering: or
> he that teacheth, on teaching; Or he that exhorteth, on
> exhortation: he that giveth, let him do it with sim-
> plicity; he that ruleth, with diligence; he that sheweth
> mercy, with cheerfulness. Let love be without dissimula-
> tion. Abhor that which is evil; cleave to that which is
> good. Be kindly affectioned one to another with broth-
> erly love; in honour preferring one another; Not slothful
> in business; fervent in spirit; serving the Lord; Rejoicing
> in hope; patient in tribulation; continuing instant in
> prayer; Distributing to the necessity of saints; given to
> hospitality. Bless them which persecute you: bless, and
> curse not. Rejoice with them that do rejoice, and weep
> with them that weep. Be of the same mind one toward
> another. Mind not high things, but condescend to men
> of low estate. Be not wise in your own conceits."*

> *I Corinthians 1:10 - "Now I beseech you, brethren, by
> the name of our Lord Jesus Christ, that ye all speak the
> same thing, and that there be no divisions among you;
> but that ye be perfectly joined together in the same
> mind and in the same judgment."*

I Corinthians 3:1-3 - "And I, brethren, could not speak unto you as unto spiritual, but as unto carnal, even as unto babes in Christ. I have fed you with milk, and not with meat: for hitherto ye were not able to bear it, neither yet now are ye able. For ye are yet carnal: for whereas there is among you envying, and strife, and divisions, are ye not carnal, and walk as men?"

All of these keys are necessary if we are to see God move in mighty ways in these days. God is going to move in a people. We can be part of what He is doing if we remain open to Him. David summarized what God is wanting to do in these days in *Psalms 102*. Notice how he refers to all three of the keys of visitation.

Psalms 102:13-22 - "Thou shalt arise, and have mercy upon Zion: for the time to favour her, yea, the set time, is come. For thy servants take pleasure in her stones, and favour the dust thereof. So the heathen shall fear the name of the Lord, and all the kings of the earth thy glory. When the Lord shall build up Zion, he shall appear in this glory. He will regard the prayer of the destitute and not despise their PRAYER. This shall be written for the generation to come: and the people which shall be created shall PRAISE the Lord. For he hath looked down from the height of his sanctuary; from heaven did the Lord behold the earth; To hear the groaning of the prisoner; to loose those that are appointed to death; To declare the name of the Lord in Zion, and his praise in Jerusalem; When THE PEOPLE ARE GATHERED TOGETHER and the kingdoms, to serve the Lord."

CONCLUSION

The writer to the Hebrews enumerates the plan and purpose of God in terms of the principles of the doctrine of Christ. These give us a picture of how God is building in these days of restoration.

Hebrews 6:1-2 - *"Therefore leaving the principles of the doctrine of Christ, let us go on to perfection; not laying again the foundation of repentance from dead works, and of faith toward God, of the doctrine of baptisms, and of laying on of hands, and of resurrection of the dead, and of eternal judgment."*

The writer enumerates the following:

1)   REPENTANCE FROM DEAD WORKS
2)   FAITH TOWARD GOD
3)   THE DOCTRINE OF BAPTISMS
4)   LAYING ON OF HANDS
5)   RESURRECTION OF THE DEAD
6)   ETERNAL JUDGMENT
7)   PERFECTION

Not only does this summarize for us what God has done, but it also gives us the direction for the future. As we remain open to the Lord, we can expect that He will accomplish His Eternal Purpose in us, and we will be established in *"the present truth" (II Peter 1:12).*

STUDY QUESTIONS FOR CHAPTER ELEVEN

1.   When was the Brazen Altar typically restored in the history of the Church?

2.   What does the changing of the priests' garments in connection with the Tabernacle of Moses typify?

3.   What does the Golden Altar of Incense typify in terms of restoration?

4.   What can we expect in the future for the Church?

5.   What are the three keys to visitation?

6)   What vehicle is God using in the present visitation?

7)   What is the key to unity? Why?

8)   What are some of the results of unity?

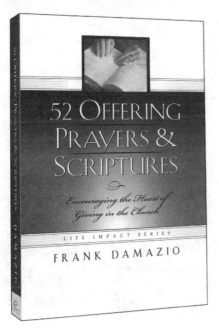

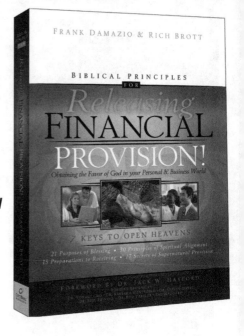

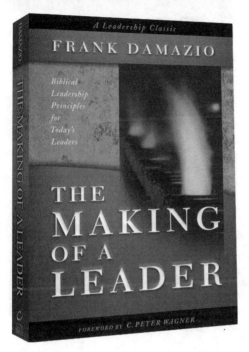

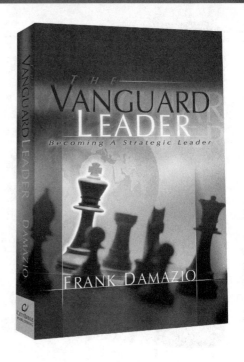

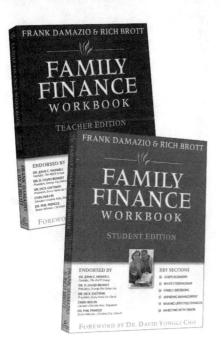

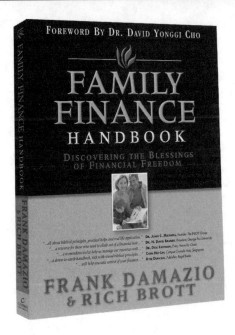